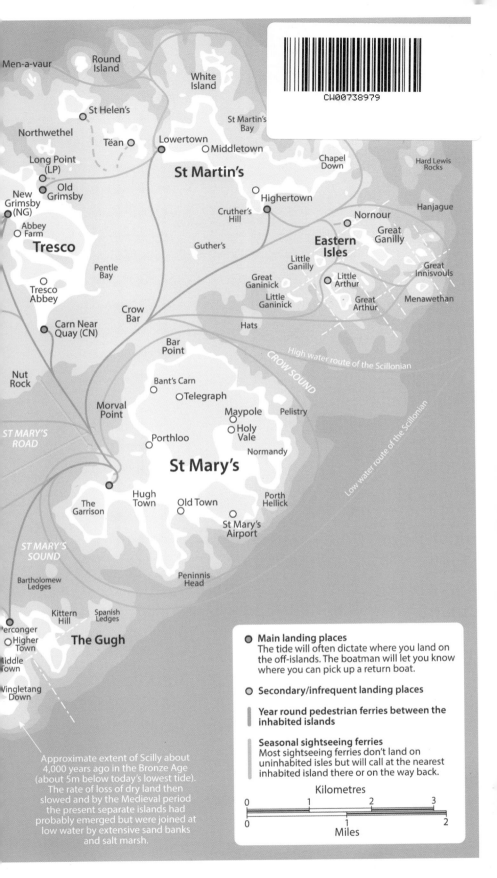

Men-a-vaur

Round Island

White Island

St Helen's

St Martin's Bay

Northwethel

Tëan

Lowertown

Middletown

Chapel Down

Hard Lewis Rocks

Long Point (LP)

Old Grimsby

St Martin's

New Grimsby (NG)

Highertown

Hanjague

Abbey Farm

Cruther's Hill

Nornour

Great Ganilly

Tresco

Guther's

Eastern Isles

Pentle Bay

Little Ganilly

Great Innisvouls

Tresco Abbey

Great Ganinick

Little Arthur

Crow Bar

Little Ganinick

Great Arthur

Menawethan

Carn Near Quay (CN)

Hats

Nut Rock

Bar Point

CROW SOUND

High water route of the Scillonian

ST MARY'S ROAD

Bant's Carn

Telegraph

Morval Point

Maypole

Pelistry

Porthloo

Holy Vale

Normandy

St Mary's

Low water route of the Scillonian

The Garrison

Hugh Town

Old Town

Porth Hellick

St Mary's Airport

ST MARY'S SOUND

Bartholomew Ledges

Peninnis Head

Kittern Hill

Spanish Ledges

Perconger

Higher Town

The Gugh

Middle Town

Wingletang Down

Approximate extent of Scilly about 4,000 years ago in the Bronze Age (about 5m below today's lowest tide). The rate of loss of dry land then slowed and by the Medieval period the present separate islands had probably emerged but were joined at low water by extensive sand banks and salt marsh.

● Main landing places
The tide will often dictate where you land on the off-islands. The boatman will let you know where you can pick up a return boat.

○ Secondary/infrequent landing places

Year round pedestrian ferries between the inhabited islands

Seasonal sightseeing ferries
Most sightseeing ferries don't land on uninhabited isles but will call at the nearest inhabited island there or on the way back.

Kilometres

| 0 | 1 | 2 | 3 |

| 0 | 1 | 2 |
Miles

CW00738979

Isles of Scilly Guidebook

St Mary's, St Agnes, Bryher, Tresco, St Martin's

By Neil Reid

EXPLORING CORNWALL AND SCILLY

No.1

Credits, acknowledgements and further reading

The following books and websites provided much of the information in this guidebook and are a good place to start for those who want to gain a more detailed picture of the islands and their history.

Cornwall Historic Environment Record

Cornish Archaeology
Cornwall Archaeological Society

**Isles of Scilly Historic Environment Research Framework:
Resource Assessment and Research Agenda**
Report by Historic Environment, Cornwall Council for English Heritage (2012)
A downloadable copy can be found on the Council of the Isles of Scilly website.

South West Archaeological Research Framework (SWARF Project)
Edited by C J Webster, Somerset County Council (2008)
A downloadable copy can be found on the Somerset County Council website.

Defending Scilly
Allan Brodie and Mark Bowden, English Heritage (2011)

The Isles of Scilly
Rosemary Parslow, The New Naturalist Library No.103 (2007)

Ships, Shipwrecks and Maritime Incidents Around the Isles of Scilly
Isles of Scilly Museum Publication No.3 (revised edition 1999)

Cornish Place-name Elements
OJ Padel, English Place-name Society Vol LVI/LVII (1985)

Exploration of a Drowned Landscape
Charles Thomas, Batsford (1985)

Ancient Scilly
Paul Ashbee, David & Charles (1974)

Cornish Shipwrecks, The Isles of Scilly
Richard Larn, David & Charles (1971)

Portrait of the Isles of Scilly
Clive Mumford, Robert Hale & Company (1967)

The Scilly Isles
Geoffrey Grigson, Routledge (1946)

Watercolour illustrations: Bridgitte Livesley

First published in 1997 as **The Map and Guide to Exploring the Isles of Scilly**
This edition © Neil Reid and Friendly Guides 2022

ISBN 978-1-904645-34-4 (Paperback)
10th Edition
No.1 in the **EXPLORING CORNWALL AND SCILLY** series

The Friendly Guides logo is a trademark of the Reid Partnership
Tel: 01736 369194 Email: sales@friendly-guides.uk
www.friendly-guides.uk

Contents

The Bar, St Agnes

Introduction

A rich sensory landscape

LIKE MANY ISLANDS, SCILLY IS SOMETHING OF AN ANTIDOTE TO life on the mainland, replacing the roar of traffic for that of the sea, trading the jostle of the daily commute for the commotion and cacophony of seabirds overhead. There is so little pollution here that at night the stars and Milky Way are fabulously clear, and as you walk along it feels as if you are being bombarded by shooting stars. For a visitor even the constraints of island life are somehow liberating, the delicious feeling of remoteness and the way that island life is dictated as much by the tide as the clock. That's not to say this is an easy place to live; those elements that so charm the visitor are real constraints for islanders and you have to be a resilient soul to deal with difficulties of island life, but to visit, Scilly is pure joy.

Of the hundreds of rocks, islets and islands on Scilly, only five are inhabited – **St Mary's** plus the off-islands of **Tresco**, **St Agnes**, **Bryher** and **St Martin's**. In the fairly recent past **Samson** was also populated, and the abandoned houses and fields are a great draw to visitors and a highlight of any visit to Scilly. Go back further in time and many other parts of Scilly were also once inhabited. A thousand years ago **St Helen's** and **Teän** were home to Early Christian communities, and a thousand years before that many of the smaller isles like **White Island** (St Martin's), **Nornour**, **Northwethel** and **Great Ganilly** were home to prehistoric farmers. Their tumbled field walls show up in the late afternoon sun as shadows in the canopy of bracken. Some of their walls run across the shore and into the sea, making dark lines under the water and inspiring tales of a past civilisation now lost to the sea – the land of Lyonesse.

St Mary's and **Tresco** are stepping stones between the mainland and the more peripheral off-islands. St Mary's even has tarmac roads and traffic (but you can't bring your car here from the mainland). It's a good base for first time visitors because all the other islands are within easy reach by ferry from Hugh Town Quay. Tresco is busy with visitors to the world famous **Abbey Gardens**, but even then you can always find a quiet corner of beach to picnic on. **St Agnes**, **Bryher** and **St Martin's** are more far-flung, distilled illustrations of island life. Here the only traffic on the small concrete tracks is an occasional tractor and a flurry of activity when a ferry arrives. Their landscapes change in the blink of an eye so that even on small isles like **Samson** and **Gugh** you move from sheltered sunny coves to wind buffeted heath and blustery tomb-topped carns in a few strides. One of the great pleasures of visiting Scilly is discovering the different characters of the islands and finding the one that appeals to your own temperament.

Granite islands of Lyonesse
A land lost beneath the sea

St Agnes from Gugh

Humans have a natural rapport with granite landscapes, reading into the odd-shaped rocks the faces of humans and the outlines of animals so that, at least in the Celtic mind, the whole landscape appears to be alive. Queen Victoria stares out from the seaward side of **The Kittern** on the northern tip of Gugh. The **Droppy Nose** rocks of Gugh and Bryher look like an elephant's head and trunk. Peninnis Head has **The Pulpit, Monk's Cowl, Toast Rack, The Claw** and **The Tooth**. Perhaps the most celebrated examples are **The Loaded Camel** at Porth Hellick (page 22) and **The Nag's Head** on St Agnes (page 42) and the list could go on. They give the cliffs, carns and downs personality.

Layout of the islands

The layout of Scilly is dictated by a system of three-dimensional cubic joints in the granite itself, mostly a result of fractures caused when the granite magma cooled and contracted deep underground (see inside front cover). The fractures are apparent both at a very large scale, in the channels that separate the islands, and at a very small scale in the shape of the rectangular blocks that crown every carn. One set of fractures run in parallel from northwest to southeast across the whole of Scilly forming deep water channels like **New Grimsby Sound** and **Crow Sound**. Superimposed at right angles is another, less pronounced set running southwest to northeast. They form the low-lying necks between Scillonian hills but also the deep channel of the **Southwest Passage** and **Broad Sound**. Taken together, this tartan grid creates the typical Scillonian landscape of roughly conical hills divided from each other by low ground and is most obvious in that

The Druid's Chair on Porth Hellick Down

most Scillonian of features – the twin-hilled island like **Samson**, **Gugh** and **The Eastern Isles**. The beautiful southwestern corner of Bryher is another good example, with its freestanding hills divided from each other by low-lying necks where great, three-quarter circle bays have been scooped out, each guarded by granite carns. The regularity of the joints is also expressed in the way that carns repeat at regular intervals, lending the coast a swinging, syncopated rhythm as you walk along the path beneath them.

Carved by Druids

On the top of many carns and scattered on the surface of downs, you'll find pitted rocks with great cups or basins large enough for a child to bathe in and some, like the **Druid's Chair**, for adults to sit in. They appear so deliberately fashioned and man-made (they're actually completely natural) that it was popularly thought they were carved by Druids to catch the blood of human sacrifices. Many of Scilly's prehistoric tombs are aligned on, and sometimes even incorporate, distinctive natural outcrops as part of their structure, so it's obvious these were important ritual places. Burial practice in long stretches of prehistory was to expose the dead, allowing the elements and wild animals to devour the flesh and pick the bones clean. Where better to expose a body than on the top of one of these distinctive carns? Stories of blood-letting might just be a distant folk memory of these excarnation or defleshing rituals from prehistory. Next time you sit on top of a carn taking in the view and eating your pasty, remember you may be only the latest of a long line of animals that have feasted here.

A land lost beneath the sea – the lost Land of Lyonesse

At the height of the last glacial period, 18,000 years ago, the sea was as much as 100 metres below today's levels, exposing a vast plain stretching all around for dozens of kilometres. As the climate warmed and the ice caps melted, huge volumes of water were released causing an astonishingly rapid rise in sea levels. At the same time, humans, who had wisely sat out the glacial period painting pictures in the caves of southern Europe, started to move north. They arrived here about 10,000 years ago to find the sea already lapping at the base of the granite hills but still a good thirty metres below today's level. By 4000BC it had risen another twenty-five metres. Even within the short life-span of prehistoric man, large areas of land could be seen to be lost to the sea. This global phenomenon is at the root of the many myths of a 'great flood'.

Generations of Scillonians have told of a lost land that once lay between the Isles of Scilly and Land's End – **The Land of Lyonesse**. A land of handsome maids and strong men, of rich pastures and fertile meadows. Standing above the fields, on what is now the **Seven Stones**, stood the beautiful **City of Lions** where from its turreted castle you could count the steeples of 140 graceful churches. All this was suddenly engulfed by the sea. Only one man and his horse survived. He was out hunting in the hills near to Land's End. Weary from his exertions, he fell asleep under a May tree only to be woken by a terrifying roar as a gigantic wave rolled across the plain from the west. He mounted his horse and they galloped for their lives to high ground and safety – but not before his horse lost a shoe in the scramble. The coat of arms of the West Cornwall Vyvyan family consists of three horseshoes and they claim to be descended from the single survivor of the flood that engulfed Lyonesse.

Sometimes late at night in the corner of a West Cornwall pub you may even overhear an old fisherman recounting stories of how on a calm day, with a still sea, you can hear a faint mournful toll as the sea currents gently move the bells in their steeples. The legend may have grown taller with every telling, but there are indeed traces of a lost society, their homes and fields now under the sea. These are the farms of Bronze Age Scillonians who colonised Scilly 4,500 years ago when the four largest present-day islands were connected by a now submerged central plain.

Possible coastline 12,000 years ago

Possible coastline 10,000 years ago

Pendeen Lighthouse

Sevenstones Lightvessel

Longships Lighthouse

Land's End

Seven Stones Reef

The City of Lions

Gwennap Head

Round Island Lighthouse

The Land of Lyonesse

ISLES OF SCILLY

Wolf Rock Lighthouse

Bishop Rock Lighthouse

Peninnis Lighthouse

Map showing the Lost Land of Lyonesse and the lighthouses around Scilly, many visible from St Martin's Head (see page 89)

The first Scillonians
Farmers and tomb builders

Entrance grave on Kittern Hill, Gugh

It's almost impossible to climb a hill on Scilly and not come across some sort of ancient tomb. Many people stand on a tomb to admire the view without realising what's under their feet. On Scilly you'll find a surprisingly complete prehistoric landscape – standing stones, Roman shrines, prehistoric field walls and even whole settlements of round huts. The granite bedrock naturally offers up blocks of convenient shape and size for construction and its inherent durability ensures that once built, they stubbornly persist even though many have been partially robbed to build later houses, farms and walls. There are archaeological tours on land and by boat; ask at the TIC for details.

Nomadic hunters – the Mesolithic (8000 – 4000BC)

We know from a few scattered finds of flint arrow heads and blades that Mesolithic people did visit Scilly. These nomadic hunters had moved north from the Mediterranean after the end of the last glacial period 12,000 years ago. At this time the climate was rapidly warming and the ice caps, which had penetrated as far south as the Bristol Channel, were in full-scale retreat. It's just possible that when people arrived here about 10,000 years ago, there was still enough water locked up in northern ice sheets that they were able to walk from Land's End or at least to use the Seven Stones Reef as a staging post to get to Scilly. What would they have found? A single large island (see map inside front cover) incorporating all of the present inhabited islands plus most of the Western Rocks and with an interior of oak, ash and hazel woods full of red deer and boar marooned here as the sea level rose. Most of their coastal camps are now long lost to the sea.

The Old Man of Gugh

Neolithic (4000 – 2500BC)

By about 6,000 years ago Scilly was separated from Land's End, and St Agnes and the Western Rocks were divided from the rest of Scilly. We know from discoveries of flint scrapers and other objects that Neolithic Stone Age hunters made camp below Cruther's Hill on St Martin's and in other places on the islands. Scilly was probably only used as a seasonal base as there's no evidence of the earliest type of Stone Age tombs, built in the centuries around 3500BC, that you see on the mainland – the large 'table' quoits such as Lanyon and Mulfra Quoit near Penzance. Farming and knowledge of cultivation reached Britain about 4000BC and penetrated Cornwall 250 to 500 years later. However, it would be another thousand years before the islands were permanently settled.

Bronze Age (2500 – 700BC)

It's possible that a shortage of land on the mainland provoked the permanent settlement of Scilly. Many Bronze Age fields in West Cornwall are laid out on exposed cliff tops and moors, which, even then, must have been marginal and unproductive land. It's as if there was pressure to cultivate every possible piece of land to feed a growing population. The first farmers on Scilly set about cutting down the wild wood and settled in groups of huts surrounded by small fields. The stone foundations of these huts are common throughout the islands and also show up as seaweed-covered circles in the sandy, shallow sea between some of the islands. Much of the best land probably lay on the low-lying plain between today's islands. A reasonable idea of the appearance of this landscape can be gathered from exploring Teän, St Helen's and Northwethel – a mosaic of dispersed farmsteads surrounded by a few fields leading up to rough pasture. It was these farmers who built the first tombs and monuments in the landscape. As well as building tombs on prominent carns and hilltops for themselves, they worked together to lay out cairns and create ritual landscapes like Shipman Head Down. Although they lived a more settled farming lifestyle than their ancestors, they must have also continued to hunt birds, seals and fish as before.

Bronze Age entrance graves and cairns

Entrance graves (sometimes referred to as passage graves or chambered tombs) are a type of Bronze Age tomb centred around a stone-lined passage set inside a circular kerbed earth platform (see page 35). They seem to have been constructed in the centuries around 2000 to 1500BC. The passage is usually just high enough to crouch in, it's often wider in the middle and the entrance is sometimes closed off by small blocking or portal stones. This type of tomb is part of a long tradition on the Atlantic seaboard and similar structures are found in Ireland, Brittany and Galicia. They are rare in most of Britain but a few examples do occur in West Cornwall, although they are far outnumbered by the more than seventy examples on Scilly. It seems this type of monument stayed in fashion for far longer here than on the mainland, where they were replaced by cairns much sooner.

Entrance graves tend to be sited on the crests of distinctive hills such as **North** and **South Hill** on Samson, **Cruther's Hill** on St Martin's and **Kittern Hill** on Gugh, but at **Porth Hellick Down** on St Mary's they're also found in groups or 'cemeteries'. We have marked them on the maps like this: ◕. The tomb at **Works Carn** on Bryher actually sits on top of a natural granite outcrop. The best examples are on St Mary's – **Innisidgen**, **Bant's Carn** and the **Giant's Grave**. Inside the passage there is evidence of collective internments over many generations both as cremations, with human remains placed in upturned pottery urns, and as simple deposition of bones (but not whole skeletons). While some examples like **Knackyboy Carn** on St Martin's held the remains of more than fifty individuals, others seem to have contained no remains at all and may have had other functions. The current thinking is to see these monuments as not only commemorative places for the dead, but also as places for the living – a prehistoric version of a shrine or parish church. The Isles of Scilly Museum displays objects recovered from excavations.

The fashion in the later Bronze Age seems to turn towards smaller earth and stone mounds called cairns. They sometimes contain a burial cist at their centre. These monuments can be difficult to spot among the jumble of natural rocks but if you keep looking your eye will become accustomed to picking out the round kerbs and square box-like cists. **Shipman Head Down** on Bryher has an exceptionally large number of cairns. Other typical Bronze Age monuments are standing stones or menhirs. The best known on Scilly is the **Old Man of Gugh**, but there are several others including the **Long Rock** near Telegraph on St Mary's.

Celts, Romans and Christians
Pirates, holy islands and hermits

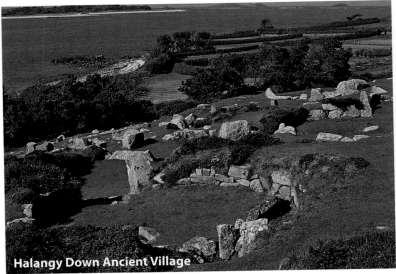

Halangy Down Ancient Village

At this time, a thousand years after the islands were first settled, the impact of rising sea levels was beginning to intrude on everyday life, although it would be another thousand years before the outline of the present-day islands was completely formed. Population levels on Scilly probably reached a peak in the later Bronze Age and early Iron Age. Many prehistoric fields are still clearly visible on the islands but are overrun by bracken or, like **Green Bay** on Bryher and on **Samson Flats**, have been swamped by the sea. The area of land under cultivation may have exceeded today's levels.

Iron Age and Romano-British (700BC – AD400)

A deterioration in the climate during the Iron Age marked the beginning of a period of increasing instability on the islands. We know that at **Halangy Down** the original Bronze Age village was overwhelmed by drifting sand and had to be relocated further up hill. Low-lying areas that had been settled by the first Bronze Age Scillonians a thousand years before must have become increasingly vulnerable to storm surges and flooding. The ocean, once a vast empty space, was now bringing trading ships from the Mediterranean and a new danger – raiders from the sea. From the 5th century BC cliff castles like the **Giant's Castle** on St Mary's and **Shipman Head Cliff Castle** on Bryher were constructed as emergency refuges for Scilly's population.

This western part of Britain had probably been acquainted with Mediterranean ships for centuries, drawn to West Cornwall to trade for its tin. The Roman invasion of Britain in the 1st century AD must have improved the security of the islands. The Romans probably had little direct impact on the day-to-day lives of people in this remote corner of Britain but there was certainly contact with Roman mariners who appear to have worshipped at a Roman shrine at **Nornour**, and a Roman altar found in Hugh Town is now in Tresco Abbey Gardens. The Nornour site is interpreted as a shrine to a part-Roman, part-Celtic sea goddess and may have been associated with a beacon for shipping. A similar beacon is thought to have stood on Land's End.

Christianity and Tavistock Abbey (AD400 – 1538)

If Roman life had little direct impact on the islands, the Christianity that accompanied it from Rome in the 4th century AD onwards, certainly did. We know Scilly was known to Rome because in AD387 two early Christian bishops, Instantius and Tibericus, were exiled here for the Priscillian heresy. They headed a cult of free love and being bishops, they insisted they got more free love, more often, than anyone else. It was rumoured at the time they bribed their way out of trouble and there's no solid evidence they actually lived here, but it does show that Scilly was on the map even if it was at the extreme edge as far away from Rome as it was possible to imagine.

Rome's retreat from Britain in AD410 precipitated a convulsion in Northern Europe and a series of mass migrations. Angles and Saxons colonised the eastern parts of Britain in turn pushing Celts westward, many leaving from the Southwest to colonise Brittany. Despite Rome's retreat, Christianity remained strong – it had taken deep root in the western fringes of Britain and Ireland. In the 6th, 7th and 8th centuries AD a tide of Irish and Welsh evangelical saints flooded over Cornwall and Scilly. They are often said to have magically crossed the sea on floating rocks, in barrels or in the case of St Ia (of St Ives), on a leaf. These Celtic holy men and women were inspired by the teachings of the 4th century Desert Fathers, hermits of the Sinai. Like the Desert Fathers they sought out remote places far from the distractions of daily life. The most famous example is Skellig Michael off the coast of County Kerry in Ireland. In Cornwall and Scilly they deliberately set up holy sanctuaries in remote coves and on isolated cliffs. Over time these sites would attract small bands of followers and after their founder's death some would continue to grow into small communities – the forerunners of the monasteries of Medieval Britain. Scilly has two fascinating examples of this, **St Theona** who lived on **Teän** and **St Elidius** who lived on **St Helen's**. Although we know very little about their lives we do still have the physical structures that were built in their sanctuaries. Other sites (and saints) existed on Scilly but have been lost. We know a sanctuary existed on Tresco near the site

Roman altar, Tresco Abbey Gardens

of the later abbey and a structure on **Samson** is now lost under the sands of **East Par**. **St Martin's** and **St Agnes** also seem to have had sites but we have no record of names and no physical remains. Presumably a knowledge of their names, life stories and sanctuaries were lost in one of the periodic bouts of depopulation on the off-islands, when the collective memory of their existence was wiped clean. Throughout this period, Scilly was plagued by the twin threats of insecurity and the loss of the best agricultural land to the rising sea; ravaged by the Vikings and with a decline in population, the islands seem to have sunk from view. After the 10th century there is little evidence that the off-islands were inhabited at all, and it may well be that the remoter parts of Scilly had few inhabitants outside these small religious communities.

Henry I (1068–1135) became king of England in 1100 and in 1120 he granted all the churches on the northern part of Scilly to the Benedictine monks of Tavistock Abbey. They set up a small monastic abbey on Tresco, helping to construct the 12th century stone chapels on Teän and St Helen's. Edward III (1312–1377) granted the islands to his son, the Black Prince, the first Duke of Cornwall and, to this day, the islands still belong to the Duchy of Cornwall. The constant menace from Vikings and sea raiders eventually forced Tavistock Abbey to abandon Tresco Abbey altogether sometime in the 14th century. When Tavistock Abbey was suppressed by Henry VIII (1491–1547) in 1538 (it's now just a few ruins in a car park), one thousand years of devotion and prayer ended with the final abandonment of the holy sites at Teän and St Helen's.

The story of Scilly is one of both being far from the centre of power, but also at certain periods being in a pivotal position on major sea routes – in prehistory, as part of the Atlantic seaboard culture, and in Roman and Early Christian times as Celtic Christianity flowed from Ireland and Wales to Cornwall and Brittany. Now, at the end of the Medieval period, it was about to come centre stage again as new worlds were discovered across the sea to the west.

Sea trade and Civil War
The world comes to Scilly

Cromwell's Castle

The growth of sea trade on the new Atlantic trade routes to America and Africa from the Tudor period onwards brought the islands to the attention of national government because now, far from being on the edge of the known world, Scilly found itself on the main trade route to The New World. For a long time Scilly was so far from the centre of power that it was effectively beyond the rule of law, a base for pirates and privateers. In an attempt to restore order and safeguard Scilly's strategic position on the new trade routes, fortifications were constructed – **Harry's Walls** on St Mary's and the **Blockhouse** on Tresco – and in 1570 the Duchy of Cornwall leased the islands to the Godolphin family in order to establish tighter control. The volume of trade passing the islands at this time can be gauged by how many of the ships ended up on the rocks and ledges of the Western Rocks, in particular, Dutch ships loaded with fabulous wealth from Brazil, the Gold Coast of Africa and India. So much silver was spilled at one site in the Western Rocks that it was named **Silver Carn**.

By Elizabethan times it wasn't just the rocks preying on shipping but also privateers based on the islands too. Piracy was ignored as long as it was to the detriment of Holland and France. The Spanish Armada of 1588 clearly illustrated how vulnerable the islands were, and so in 1593 Elizabeth I ordered the construction of the **Star Castle** on the Garrison. But just as Scilly's prospects were improving, the event that had been threatening throughout Scillonian history finally happened, and the single prehistoric isle that had existed since 4000BC was finally split into the outline of today's off-islands by rising sea levels.

On the lowest tides of the year it's still possible to wade between Samson, Tresco and Bryher

English Civil War (1642–1651)

Scilly was staunchly Royalist during the Civil War and the young Prince Charles, later Charles II, stayed briefly in the Star Castle on his flight from the Parliamentary forces in 1646. After the Star Castle was captured by Parliament there was a brief peace until 1648 when the islands rebelled and took up privateering again, attacking any passing merchantman they could find. The toll on Dutch shipping prompted the Dutch Fleet to declare war on the islands in 1651 – an act that was only formally withdrawn in 1986 when the Dutch ambassador visited the islands to conclude a peace treaty. All over the islands you'll come across small levelled gun platforms and battery positions from this time – **Carn of Works** on the south end of Gugh, around the **Garrison** and **Works Point** on Bryher among many.

At the end of the Civil War, in order to dilute Scilly's Royalist sympathies, Parliament encouraged a period of resettlement by families from the mainland. Many Cornish place-names seem to have been lost from the collective memory during the various periods of abandonment, so this new wave of people brought English place-names with them like Grimsby and Dolphin (Godolphin) on Tresco and a puritan straightforwardness in naming settlements as Lowertown, Middletown and Highertown on St Agnes and St Martin's. Some old Cornish names did survive on the coast, kept alive by fishermen and mariners, so even in the Western Rocks we have Crebawethan, Illiswilgig and Melledgan – meaty Cornish words to wrap your tongue around. At this time visitors to the islands often commented how cosmopolitan and well spoken the islanders were from their close contact with sea trade, a stark contrast to the people of West Cornwall, many of whom spoke only Cornish.

18th century to today

The wars with France disrupted smuggling and fishing, both major sources of income for Scillonians. A series of poor harvests following the end of the Napoleonic wars brought a real prospect of famine on Scilly and life was again at a low ebb. Pilotage fees for ships sailing to the major British ports gave some relief but it was not enough to stop the islands falling into destitution. The Godolphin family relinquished their lease on the islands in 1831 and it fell to a visionary man called Augustus Smith to turn the situation around. He obtained the lease from the Duchy of Cornwall in 1834 and set about reform, funding the building of schools and insisting that the children should be well educated. New agricultural practices were introduced including the growing of flowers for the city markets and developing tourism. This humane and far-sighted approach revitalised the poverty-struck islands. The growth of the railways in the middle of the 19th century brought the first tourists to the islands from Cornwall and also allowed the flower industry to flourish. For the first time cut flowers could now reach the London markets within a day, and Scilly could exploit its early flowering season by supplying the London markets in the winter.

Political instability in Europe at the beginning of the 20th century caused the government, ever mindful of the islands strategic position, to build new coastal batteries on the Garrison, and during World War I flying boats were stationed at Tresco. Augustus Smith's family gave up the lease of the islands in the 1930s retaining only Tresco where they continue to develop and care for the gardens. Today, most of the islands are leased to the Isles of Scilly Wildlife Trust and tourism is more important than ever. Many visitors return over and over finding Scilly to be an irresistible combination of ingredients – an animated granite landscape, a prehistoric land lost to the sea and a place where the senses come alive.

Cannon from the wreck of *HMS Association* on display at Valhalla in Tresco Abbey Gardens

Crow Pole, looking over to St Helen's and Round Island from St Mary's

1. St Mary's

Scilly's mainland

ST MARY'S IS THE LARGEST ISLAND IN THE Scillonian group and home to three-quarters of Scilly's 2,200 residents. It is a stepping stone between the mainland and the off-islands, large enough to have tarmac roads, cars and buses but small enough to walk around in a day. All the off-islands are within easy reach by ferry from the quay at **Hugh Town**, so it's the ideal place to be based on your first trip. Almost all St Mary's food shops, banks, restaurants and gift shops are based here.

It's perfectly possible to walk the whole coast of St Mary's in a single day (it's about 12.5km not including the Garrison) but it's probably more enjoyable to put your holiday head on and wander along at Scillonian pace. It's amazing what you come across on the coast path – the buckled steel plates of the *SS Brodfield* on the rocks below the airport, a pillbox disguised as a wall at **Old Town**, Civil War batteries, a smuggler's cache in the cliff at **Porth Mellon** and at **Porth Hellick** and **Normandy** downs the tombs of prehistoric Scillonians.

There are two popular walks from Hugh Town: one follows the coast from **Porthcressa** to **Peninnis Head** and the other traces a line around the walls of **The Garrison**. The rest of St Mary's coastline can be split into several easy sections: Old Town to Porth Hellick, Porth Hellick to Watermill Cove and Watermill Cove to Porthloo. You can turn inland at any one of these places to make a circular walk using the country lanes and nature trails at **Lower** and **Higher Moors** to cross the island. Each walk only takes a morning or an afternoon to complete and so a pair of walks can be put together based around lunch at one of the cafes on the north of St Mary's. Alternatively, you can hire a bicycle in Hugh Town or arrange for a taxi to drop you off at **Telegraph** or **Pelistry** and saunter back along the coast path. Many visitors will understandably spend the bulk

OFF-ISLAND FERRIES
Depart from Hugh Town Quay to all parts of Scilly. Check social media and chalk boards in Hugh Town for times and destinations.

INFORMATION
Tourist Information Centre at Porthcressa for information on where to go and what to do. Email info@visitislesofscilly.com
T: (01720) 620600
www.visitislesofscilly.com

TAXIS AND BIKE HIRE
St Mary's Bike Hire
The Strand, Hugh Town.
07552 994 709
The Scilly Cart Co
Electric carts for exploring St Mary's. Porthmellon Business Park.
T: (01720) 422121
DJ Cabs
T: (01720) 423775
M: 07717 121 101
Toots Taxis
T: (01720) 422142
M: 07570 624 669

PLACES TO VISIT
- Isles of Scilly Museum
- Buzza Tower Camera Obscura
- Holy Vale Wines

BEACHES
Porthcressa is good for families, **Pelistry** is the most popular.

The Loaded Camel at Porth Hellick

of their time exploring the coast, but the centre of St Mary's has plenty to offer too. It's mainly cultivated for potatoes, flowers and bulbs – particularly daffodils and other narcissi which are sent to London in the winter and early spring. **Holy Vale** is a particularly beautiful spot with vineyards where you can try out the local Pinot Noir (check opening times before you go). You'll also come across artists studios, potteries and galleries like **Rocky Hill** and the studios at **Porthloo**.

St Mary's has many impressive prehistoric monuments and, if you're interested in the ancient history of the islands, it's a good plan to spend a bit of time visiting sites like the **Giant's Tomb** on Porth Hellick Down, **Innisidgen Tomb** and **Bant's Carn Tomb** at Halangy Down. They are kept clear of bracken and brambles and have information boards so that when you get to the off-islands – whose ancient sites are often a little tumbled down and overgrown – you already have a clear picture in your own mind of what you're looking for among all the natural rock debris. The northern part of St Mary's around the **The Bar** and **Halangy Down** was intensively settled in prehistory and the remains of prehistoric fields, huts and tombs show that this part of Scilly, facing back to Land's End, was probably the major centre of activity on ancient Scilly. A well-preserved prehistoric village at **Halangy Down** has been excavated and you can wander around the remains of 2,000-year-old houses and explore the older tomb at nearby Bant's Carn.

For nature lovers, there are lots of wildlife boat trips from the quay at Hugh Town including one on a glass-bottomed boat as well as lectures in the Church Hall in Hugh Town. The island has a good variety of resident birds, and **Porth Hellick Pool** is a favourite spot in the spring and autumn for migrating birds who stop here to rest and refuel. Sometimes when gales blow in exotic birds from North America, hundreds of birdwatchers descend on the islands. They can be found crouching in hedgerows and craning their necks over walls to catch sight of unusual visitors. Naturalist Will Wagstaff leads half and full day walks around the islands (Island Wildlife Tours).

Hugh Town, the Garrison, Old Town and Peninnis Head

Buzza Tomb, looking over Hugh Town and Porthcressa

Hugh Town is the bustling hub of Scilly – all the off-island ferries leave from the quay here, as does as the *Scillonian*, signalling its imminent arrival or departure with long blasts on its horn. The sheltered beach at **Porthcressa** is very popular with families in the summer with loos, cafes and shops all within easy reach. **The Garrison** dominates the town with its impressive defences, an almost continuous line of batteries, redans and walls built over 400 years, starting with the **Star Castle** and ending with the early 20th century coastal gun batteries designed to defend the island from bombardment from the sea.

Hugh Town and Harry's Walls

The growing importance of sea trade in the Tudor period and the strategic position of Scilly on the new Atlantic trade routes to America and Africa brought the islands to the attention of national government. In order to safeguard Scilly a fort was started in 1550 at Harry's Walls above Porth Mellon. New theories on gunnery angles and arcs of fire were used in the design of the bastion walls, but the site itself was poorly chosen and gave only very limited protection to shipping in St Mary's Road. It was abandoned before completion and the focus then shifted to fortifying the whole headland or hugh (Cornish *ughel* for *high place*) that would become The Garrison. The building of the Star Castle in the 1590s shifted the whole island's centre of gravity away from Old Town to this narrow neck below the new fortifications. Its location here is a little precarious and even within living memory, there have been times when waves have washed all the way across from Porthcressa to Town Beach through the streets.

The Star Castle and the Garrison

The Star Castle was started in 1593 in response to the Spanish Armada of 1588 which, despite its failure, nevertheless highlighted Scilly's acute vulnerability to attack. A geometric design was used, based on the castles constructed by Henry VIII (1491–1547) along the south coast of England from Deal in Kent to Pendennis Castle at Falmouth. The Garrison walls overlooking the town were built during the reign of Elizabeth I (1533–1603) and were progressively extended in fits and starts until 1750, by which time the whole headland with the exception of a small stretch around Doctor's Keys, was effectively fortified. Ships have to sail close to Woolpack Point to avoid the Spanish and Bartholomew Ledges that sit mid-channel in St Mary's Sound. The gun platforms and batteries are sited close to the water so that they could send their shot bouncing and skimming across the surface of the water. You may hear the bell of the Spanish Ledges Buoy as you walk along the path from Morning Point. At Woolpack Point a path climbs up the hill to Woolpack Battery, an early 20th century Coastal Defence Battery, and one of a series of batteries around the British coast that were built around 1900 in response to political instability and revolution in Europe. All were rendered obsolete by the use of the first atomic bomb in 1945.

Old Town and Peninnis Head

The main seat of Norman civil administration was at the now demolished Ennor Castle at Old Town. All that's left now is a kink as the road makes a diversion around the mound. Old Town Bay or Porthennor, as it was then known, was the main landing place on Scilly. Tavistock Abbey (who had daughter churches on Scilly) established the church here sometime after AD1100. Peninnis Head has a famously exotic collection of odd-shaped rocks – it's almost hallucinatory – look out for the Monk's Cowl, Toast Rack, Kettles and Pans, Pulpit Rock, the Tooth, the Turtle and the Claw. The lighthouse was erected in 1911 (1 white flash every 20 seconds) and superseded the old lighthouse on St Agnes.

Map labels: Kitty O'Flanagh 1838; Newman Rock; Store House Battery; King Charles' Battery; Pottery; Barrel of Butter; Garrison; The Star Castle Hotel; Independenza 1881; Doctor's Keys; Triumph 1736; Hugh House; Steval Point; The Steval; Battery; Searchlight position and pillbox; Steval Battery Early C20th; Garrison Farm; Colonel George Boscawen's Battery; Woolpack Battery Early C20th; Bartholomew Battery; Blazer 1918; Searchlight control position; Mercurias 1835; Serica Rock; SS Serica 1893; Searchlight position; Woolpack Point; The Woolpack; Britannia 1753; ST MARY'S SOUND

TO HALANGY DOWN PREHISTORIC
VILLAGE AND BANT'S CARN

BAR POINT

Telegraph

Telegraph
Tower

Lower
Newford
Farm

Watermill

Carn Morval
Down

val Point
*Borodino
1830*

Civil War
Battery

Isles of Scilly
Golf Club

Content
Farm

HIGH LANE

n Morval

*La Maria Clara
1780*

Club
House

Silver
Carn

TOWN LANE

PUNGIES

Taylor's
Island

Juliet's
Garden

Seaways Farm

PORTHLOO LANE

Holy Vale

PELISTRY

Calf

ow

Porthlow Farm

Trewince

TELEGRAPH ROAD

HOLY VALE LANE

*Longstone-
Holyvale
footpath*

*Gem 1881
Boiler visible
at low water*

Porthloo

Centre

Longstone
Farm

A3110

*Tuck 1863
ad in Valhalla
m on Tresco*

Old
Quay

Boat
Yard

Longstone

PORTH LOO LN

Studios

Porthloo
Pool

Sunnyside

Four
Lanes
End

Longstone
Terrace

Newford
Island

ROCKY HILL LN

PORTH HELLICK,
NORMANDY

Shark's Pit
(Thomas' Porth)

Mount
Flagon

Rocky Hill
Farm

Carreg
Dhu

Garden

ST MARY'S
POOL

Smuggler's cache in cliff

Menhir
Harry's
Walls

PUMP LN

Tre

Lifeboat
Station

Porth
Mellon

Rosehill

A3111

Hugh
Town

Carn
Thomas

Shooters
(Low) Pool

Parting
Carn

A3112

Town
Beach

IND EST

Phoenix
Craft

Sandy
Banks

Pottery

Scented
Narcissi

CHURCH ST

Moor
Well

Lower
Moors

AIRPORT (HIGH CROSS) LN

Airport
Bungalows

STRAND

Dump

Bird
Hide

PAGE 29

JACKSON'S HILL

MOORWELL LANE

Nature
Trail

PORTHCRESSA RD

Entrance
grave

Buzza
Tower

Doyley
Woods

Site of
Ennor
Castle

ENNOR CLOSE

Old
Town

St Mary's
Airport

Little Carn
Porthcressa
Beach

Buzza
Hill

Carn
Gwaval

Five
Islands
School

*Hidden
Pillbox*

CHURCH ROAD

Hospital
& Health
Centre

PELISTRY RETREAT

row
eeze

Allotments

Peninnis
House

Nowhere

Slip

Tolman
Carns

Porth
Minick

PORTH HELLICK

orthcressa

KING EDWARDS RD

Peninnis
Farm

Old Quay

Inner Bl
Carn

*Pilchard
Pool*

Porthcressa
Brow

Old Town
Bay

Mainmark
Rock

Outer
Blue Carn
*Bro
(steel
between*

ng

Raveen

Carn Lêh

Gull
Rock

Tolman
Point

Fennel

Nicholls
Rock

Stony
Porth

*Windmill
(ruin)*

Joe's Rock

*Gilstone
Ledges*

The
Wras

*Named after
Capt. William
Nicholls lost on
this rock 1738*

Carn
Mahael

Carn Lêh
Cove

Biggal

Dutchman's Carn

Kettle
and Pans

Pulpit Rock

Peninnis
Head

The Chair

Tooth
Rock

Piper's Hole

Carrickstarne

Old Town
Gilstone

The Murrs

*Criccieth
Castle 1883*

Monk's
Cowl

Izzicumpucca

Inner Head

Inner
Basin

Little Jolly Rock

Pollard

*Roch Castle
1911*

Big Jolly Rock

Outer
Head

*Minnehaha
1874*

These two pleasant strolls are both within easy reach of Hugh Town. The Garrison stroll is a good way to get your bearings on Scilly as all the other islands are visible from up here. Peninnis is good at any time of day but is particularly popular in the evening and when the sea is rough.

Peninnis Head

Garrison stroll

A walk full of interest for the multiperiod batteries and gun emplacements but also for anyone who wants to enjoy the views over St Mary's Sound to St Agnes and the Bishop Rock Lighthouse. You can stop at The Star Castle Hotel or Tregarthen's Hotel for refreshments.

From **The Bank** in Hugh Town, the main access is up **Garrison Hill** and past **Tregarthen's Hotel**. Once through the **Garrison Gate** you can walk in either direction around the Garrison walls. Most people turn south and walk past **Hugh House**. There's also foot access from **Porthcressa** through the **Sally Port**. You can walk outside the south-facing walls from **Morning Point**

and this is a sunny place to sit for a picnic. Listen out for the bell buoy marking the Spanish Ledges. At **Woolpack Battery** there are good views over to Gugh and St Agnes past **Woolpack Beacon** and the red and black mark on **Bartholomew Ledges**. Follow the coast to **Steval Point** and back to the **Garrison Gate**. English Heritage publish a book called *Defending Scilly* that has lots of pictures and information on the evolution of the Garrison and its defences – it's available from the Paper Shop.

Distance
2.4km (1½ miles) following the wall.
Places to picnic
Any sunny corner in front of the walls from Morning Point to Steval Point.

Peninnis Head/ Porthloo

A popular evening stroll. Children love the unusual rock formations. Easily extended to take in Old Town, Lower Moors Nature Trail and Porthloo.

Follow the coast path from the east end of **Porthcressa Beach** below **Buzza Hill** and through the allotments to **Peninnis Head**. You have several options here. To return to Hugh Town by the shortest route, follow **King Edward's Road**. For a longer walk follow the coast path to **Carn Lêh** and **Old Town**. Now take **Trench Lane** to **Lower Moors Nature Trail**. When you come to the main road, turn left for Hugh Town or follow the minor road to **Porthloo** and **Juliet's Garden Cafe** where you can sit out on the terrace and enjoy the views. Then return to **Hugh Town** on the coast path to **Porthloo** and **Harry's Walls**.

Distance
3.2km (2 miles) Porthcressa to Peninnis and back via King Edward's Road.
5.6km (3½ miles) from Porthcressa to Peninnis, Old Town, Lower Moors, Juliet's Garden, Porthloo and back to Hugh Town.
Places to picnic and swim
Swim at Porthcressa or Porth Mellon. Picnic at Carn Lêh or Harry's Walls.

Woolpack Battery

Porth Hellick, Higher Moors, Pelistry and Holy Vale

Porth Hellick

Two wide bays mark the start and end of this section. **Porth Hellick** is the starting point for **The Higher Moors Nature Trail** that meanders up the valley to the beautiful vineyards at **Holy Vale**. **Pelistry Bay** is St Mary's favourite beach. The cliffs between them are a little less windswept than those of The Garrison and Peninnis Head. Even so, they are exposed enough to have remained uncultivated for hundreds of metres inland from the edge of the cliff. This zone has always been difficult to cultivate but was clearly an important ritual place in prehistory. Both **Porth Hellick** and **Normandy** downs are peppered with tombs, including the famous **Giant's Grave** as well as odd-shaped natural rocks like the **Druid's Chair** and the **Twin Sisters**.

The Giant's Castle and Porth Hellick

Cliff castles are a feature of the whole Cornish coast and seem to date from around the 1st to 5th centuries BC. Here at the Giant's Castle, four earth and stone banks with a staggered entrance gap defend the steeply rising and rocky cliff top. These don't seem to have been permanent settlements – they're just too exposed and they rarely have a water supply. It's more likely that they were temporary refuges in response to threats and raids from the sea. Similar earth and stone ramparts occur on Shipman Head on Bryher and Burnt Hill on St Martin's. Judging from the concentration of monuments that flank the constrained entrance to Porth Hellick Bay, this appears to have been an important place in prehistory. Today it's a very quiet and peaceful place where you can wade in the shallows and rock pools and admire the Loaded Camel Rock (photo page 22).

Cloudesley Shovell is smothered

A small memorial plaque stands just above the beach at Porth Hellick. It's to Admiral Sir Cloudesley Shovell who, along with a substantial part of the British Fleet, was wrecked on the Western Rocks in 1707 (page 48). Sir Cloudesley was washed ashore here, barely alive, along with the dead bodies of his two step children, their pet dog and another naval officer. They must have made it to a ship's boat or clung to some wreckage because Porth Hellick is twelve kilometres from the Western Rocks. At that time it was lawful to remove objects from a corpse washed up on a beach but not to take things from the living who made it to shore. Sir Cloudesley was found by a local woman who, seeing a large emerald ring on his finger, suffocated him by smothering his face with her skirt, something she admitted only on her deathbed many years later. He was buried above the shore temporarily and soon after, his body was dug up, embalmed in a barrel of French brandy, carried to London and he now lies in Westminster Abbey.

Higher Moors Nature Trail and Holy Vale

At the back of Porth Hellick you can leave the coast altogether and walk inland past Porth Hellick Pool. It's fed by one of the very few freshwater streams on Scilly and provides much of the drinking water for St Mary's. The Higher Moors Nature Trail wanders around the reed beds, once used for making wicker crab pots, crosses the road and continues through the marshy elm woods to Holy Vale, one of the few truly sheltered places on the islands. The elms here have survived isolated from Dutch elm disease that killed so many trees on the mainland. The vineyards at Holy Vale were planted in 2009. The small visitor centre and shop is usually open in the afternoon and also hosts evening wine tasting events (check opening times first).

Porth Hellick Down, Normandy, Mount Todden and Pelistry Bay

Go past the Loaded Camel Rock and up onto Porth Hellick Down, a Bronze Age ritual landscape thick with entrance graves, the best of which, the Giant's Grave, is an unusually large and very fine example having been excavated and reconstructed in the early 20th century. Look out for the Druid's Chair too. A little further on at Normandy Down, three entrance graves stand in a line next to a very large white arrow. Aircraft in World War II used the arrow to mark the start of bombing runs on practice targets anchored in Crow Sound. Mount Todden is a curious battery and watch post possibly reusing some granite slabs from a prehistoric tomb. Lastly, you come to Pelistry Bay, probably the best beach on St Mary's, and it's a chance to get refreshments at nearby Carn Vean Cafe.

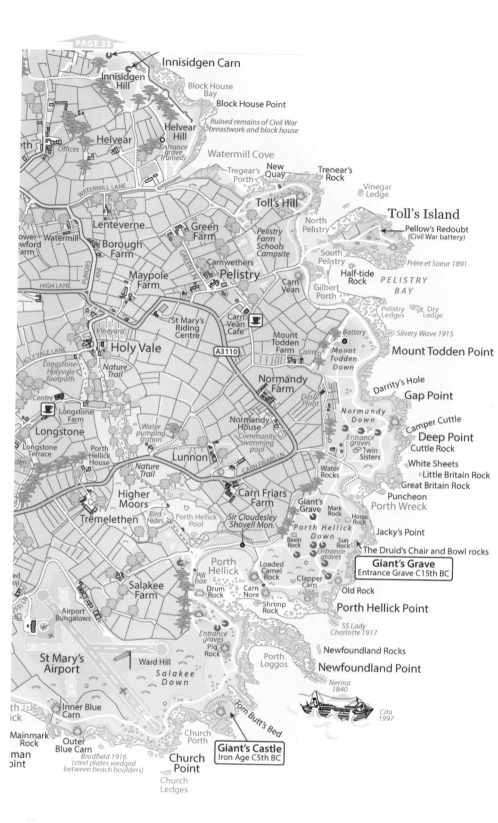

Innisidgen Carn

Innisidgen Hill

Block House Bay

Block House Point

Ruined remains of Civil War breastwork and block house

Helvear Hill

Helvear

Offices

Entrance grave (ruined)

Watermill Cove

Tregear's Porth

New Quay

Trenear's Rock

Vinegar Ledge

Toll's Hill

Toll's Island

Lenteverne

Green Farm

Pelistry Farm Schools Campsite

North Pelistry

Pellow's Redoubt (Civil War battery)

Frère et Soeur 1891

WATERMILL LANE

Lower-Newford Farm

Watermill

Borough Farm

Carnwethers

South Pelistry

Half-tide Rock

PELISTRY BAY

HIGH LANE

Maypole Farm

Pelistry

Carn Vean

Gilbert Porth

Pelistry Ledges

Dry Ledge

St Mary's Riding Centre

Carn Vean Cafe

Battery

Silvery Wave 1915

Holy Vale

Vineyard

A3110

Mount Todden Farm

Cairn

Mount Todden Down

Mount Todden Point

HOLY VALE LANE

Longstone-Holyvale footpath

Nature Trail

Darrity's Hole

Gap Point

Centre

Longstone Farm

Normandy Farm

Desal Plant

Normandy Down

Camper Cuttle

Deep Point

Cuttle Rock

Longstone

Longstone Terrace

Porth Hellick House

Water pumping station

Normandy House

Community swimming pool

Entrance graves

Twin Sisters

White Sheets

Little Britain Rock

Great Britain Rock

Lunnon

Nature Trail

CARN FRIARS LN

Water Rocks

Puncheon

Porth Wreck

Higher Moors

Tremelethen

Bird Hides

Porth Hellick Pool

Sir Cloudesley Shovell Mon.

Carn Friars Farm

Giant's Grave

Mark Rock

Horse Rock

Porth Hellick Down

Jacky's Point

The Druid's Chair and Bowl rocks

Giant's Grave
Entrance Grave C15th BC

Porth Hellick

Pill box

Basin Rock

Sun Rock

Entrance graves

Loaded Camel Rock

Clapper Carn

Old Rock

Porth Hellick Point

Salakee Farm

Drum Rock

Carn Nore

Shrimp Rock

SS Lady Charlotte 1917

Airport Bungalows

Entrance graves

Pig Rock

Porth Loggos

Newfoundland Rocks

Newfoundland Point

Nerina 1840

St Mary's Airport

Ward Hill

Salakee Down

Tom Butt's Bed

Cita 1997

Inner Blue Carn

Church Porth

Giant's Castle
Iron Age C5th BC

Mainmark Rock

Outer Blue Carn

Brodfield 1916 (steel plates wedged between beach boulders)

Church Point

Church Ledges

Looking over Porth Hellick to The Loaded Camel

Holy Vale, Porth Hellick and Pelistry

Lots to see and sample on this side of St Mary's. Funny shaped granite carns – Loaded Camel, Pig, Horse and Drum Rocks plus a Druid's Chair. Local wines to sample at Holy Vale and prehistoric tombs on Porth Hellick Down as well as the best beach on St Mary's at Pelistry. A good walk straight from landing at St Mary's Airport if you're over on a day trip from Land's End. It's a 2.7km (1¾ mile) walk to Holy Vale from the quay at Hugh Town if you're arriving from an off-island and a 5km (2¾ mile) walk from Porth Hellick back to Hugh Town Quay along the coast, 3.8km (2¼ miles) if you decide to miss out the coast path around Peninnis Head.

We'll start from **Holy Vale** in this circular walk. You can get there from **Hugh Town** by taxi or by walking along the coast. Alternatively, walk along the road to **Porth Mellon**, turn left at Rosehill and then right along **Rocky Hill Lane** to **Four Lanes** and **Holy Vale**. From here, wander past the vines and follow the **Holy Vale Nature Trail** down to **Porth Hellick Pool**. There are bird hides on the pool's edge. Follow the coast path past **The Loaded Camel** and up on to **Porth Hellick Down**. The inland paths across the down will take you to the **Giant's Grave**. Return to the coast to sit in the **Druid's Chair**. Continue over **Normandy**

Down and then inland up to **Mount Todden Battery** – an odd construction, part a possible prehistoric tomb, part Civil War battery. Then onto **Pelistry** and a swim or, turn up the lane to **Carn Vean Cafe**. The coast path at **Pelistry** is on the beach itself. Continue around **Toll's Hill** and **Trenear's Rock**, a popular place for shags and cormorants to dry out their wings between diving for fish. **New Quay** is a typical Scillonian quay still used by fishermen landing lobsters and crabs. Above **Tregear's Porth** the path turns uphill for a few hundred metres and away from the coast. Then turn left along the track that runs parallel to the coast and on to **Watermill Cove**. Return to **Holy Vale** along **Watermill Lane** and **Pungies Lane**.

Distance
The walk itself from Holy Vale to Porth Hellick, Pelistry, Watermill Cove and back is 5.1km/2¾ miles.
Best picnic spots
Under the carns at Porth Hellick Point, Pelistry Bay.

Higher Moors

Watermill Cove, Innisidgen, Crow Bar and Halangy Down

The *Scillonian* rounds Bar Point, Tresco Abbey is in the background

The coast now starts to mellow as it turns away from the open sea. The cliffs are lower and more sheltered, eventually melting away altogether into the sand dunes at **Bar Point**. This is a peaceful part of St Mary's far from the hubbub of Hugh Town and closer to the mood of the off-islands. As you come around the top of the island the Eastern Isles come into view across **Crow Sound** followed by St Martin's and Tresco. One of the great pleasures of this coast is sitting on **Innisidgen Carn** and watching the ferries come and go between the off-islands and Hugh Town. Just before noon the *Scillonian* steams into view* coming close-in to avoid the **Hats Ledges**. For a ship that looks so big when you pass her berthed in Hugh Town Harbour, she looks tiny set against the Eastern Isles. As we'll see, this area was well populated in prehistory and you will come across not just the tombs, but also the fields and, at **Halangy Down Ancient Village**, the settlements of the first Scillonians.

Watermill Cove, Innisidgen Carn and tombs

Unusually for Scilly, whose bays are mostly broad and sandy, Watermill Cove is a narrow inlet. It's a beautiful spot in the morning sun and a lovely place to swim when the tide is up. Two fine entrance graves stand near Innisidgen Carn. Their siting is unusual as most tombs are set on high ground well above or away from cultivated areas. It's likely that when the tombs were built here they did sit well above contemporary fields but these have now been lost under sea and sand.

---

* *If it's low water, the Scillonian can't clear Crow Bar and instead follows the coast south around Peninnis and The Garrison – see inside front cover.*

Bar Point and Crow Bar – the old land link to the off-islands

Crow Bar is the place where, from prehistory into the early Medieval period, a land bridge connected St Mary's to Tresco, Bryher and St Martin's making them into a single island – the old Isle of Ennor. There have long been stories of an old paved road running beneath the sand from Bar Point to Craggyellis and Guther's Island and from there to Tresco and St Martin's. Today when the tide is out, it's still too shallow for the *Scillonian* to clear Crow Bar. The area around Halangy Down, Pendrathen and Bar Point was well cultivated and settled in prehistory, and the traces of prehistoric huts and boulder field walls cover Halangy Down and lie under the dunes at Bar Point.

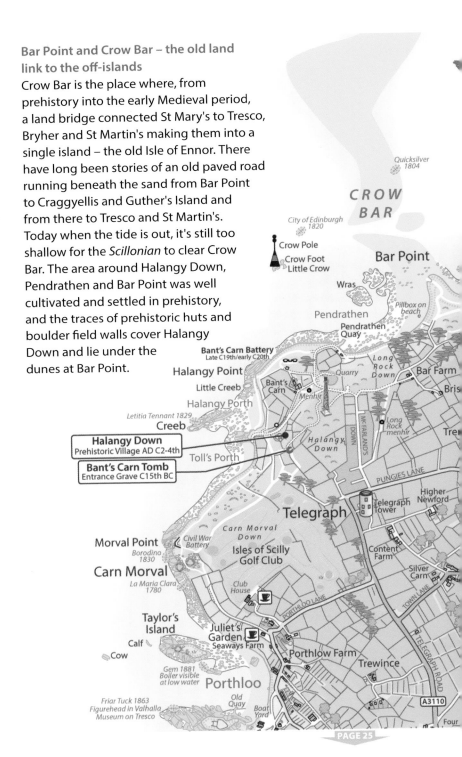

Quicksilver 1804

CROW BAR

City of Edinburgh 1820

Crow Pole
Crow Foot
Little Crow

Bar Point

Wras

Pendrathen

Pillbox on beach

Pendrathen Quay

Bant's Carn Battery
Late C19th/early C20th

Long Rock Down

Bar Farm

Halangy Point

Quarry

Little Creeb

Bant's Carn

Menhir

Bris

Halangy Porth

Letitia Tennant 1829

Creeb

Long Rock menhir

Tre

Halangy Down
Prehistoric Village AD C2-4th

Halangy Down

MC FARLAND'S DOWN

Toll's Porth

Bant's Carn Tomb
Entrance Grave C15th BC

PUNGIES LANE

Higher Newford

Telegraph Tower

Telegraph

Carn Morval Down

Morval Point

Civil War Battery

Isles of Scilly Golf Club

Content Farm

Borodino 1830

Silver Carn

Carn Morval

La Maria Clara 1780

Club House

TOWN LANE

Taylor's Island

Juliet's Garden

Seaways Farm

Porthlow Farm

Trewince

Calf

PORTHLOO LANE

Cow

Gem 1881
Boiler visible at low water

Porthloo

Old Quay

TELEGRAPH ROAD

Friar Tuck 1863
Figurehead in Valhalla Museum on Tresco

Boat Yard

A3110

Four

PAGE 25

It looks as if this area, like the original Bronze Age village at Halangy Porth, was overwhelmed by drifting sand dunes some time around 1000BC. The sand has even preserved plough marks on the ancient soil surface.

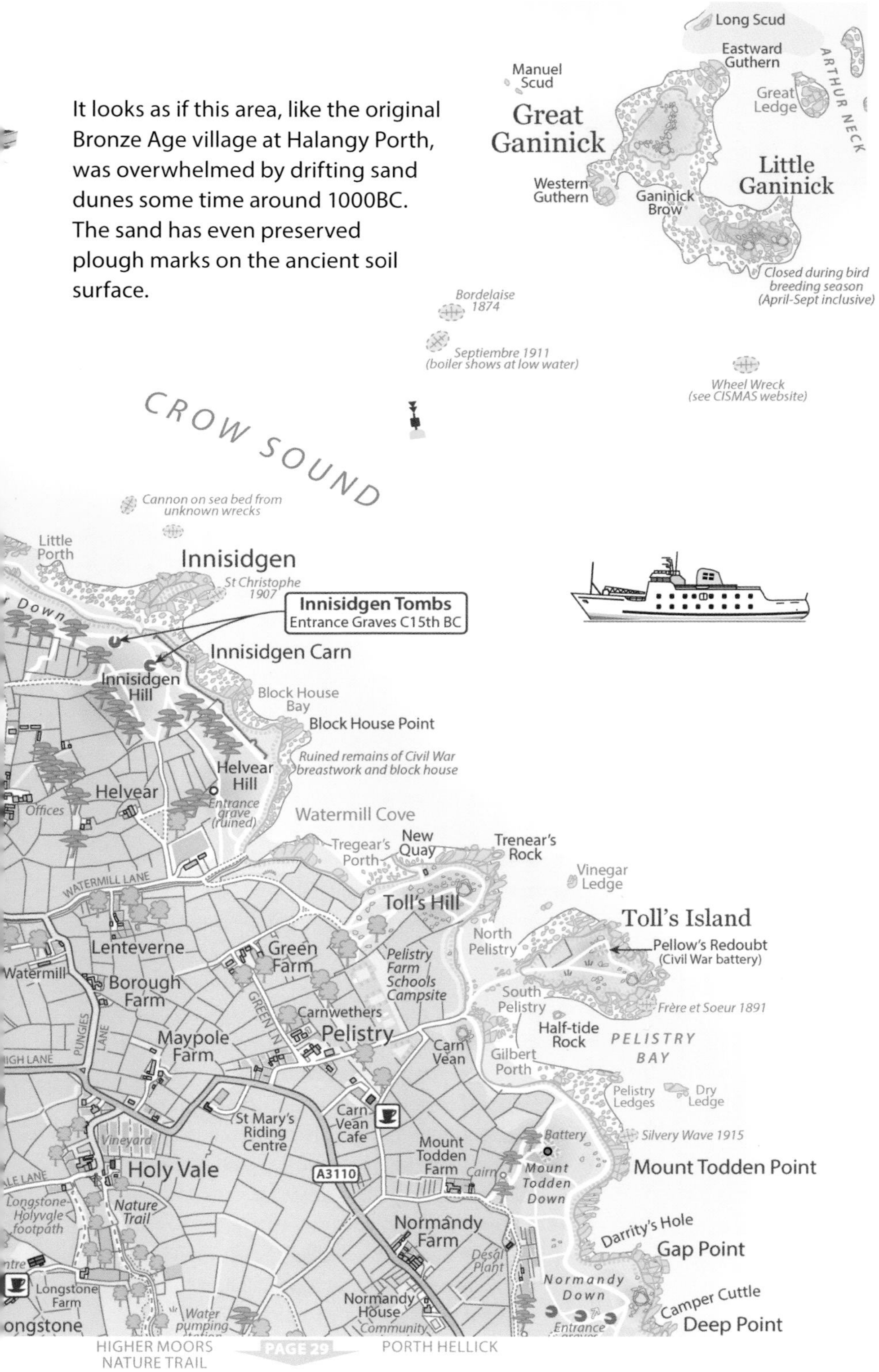

Long Scud

Eastward Guthern

ARTHUR NECK

Manuel Scud

Great Ganinick

Great Ledge

Little Ganinick

Western Guthern

Ganinick Brow

Closed during bird breeding season (April-Sept inclusive)

Bordelaise 1874

Septiembre 1911 (boiler shows at low water)

Wheel Wreck *(see CISMAS website)*

CROW SOUND

Cannon on sea bed from unknown wrecks

Little Porth

Down

Innisidgen

St Christophe 1907

Innisidgen Tombs
Entrance Graves C15th BC

Innisidgen Carn

Innisidgen Hill

Block House Bay

Block House Point

Helvear Hill

Ruined remains of Civil War breastwork and block house

Entrance grave (ruined)

Helvear

Offices

Watermill Cove

Tregear's Porth

New Quay

Trenear's Rock

Vinegar Ledge

WATERMILL LANE

Toll's Hill

North Pelistry

Toll's Island

Pellow's Redoubt (Civil War battery)

Lenteverne

Green Farm

Pelistry Farm Schools Campsite

South Pelistry

Frère et Soeur 1891

Watermill

Borough Farm

GREEN LN

Carnwethers

Pelistry

Half-tide Rock

PELISTRY BAY

HIGH LANE

PUNGIES LANE

Maypole Farm

Carn Vean

Gilbert Porth

Pelistry Ledges

Dry Ledge

St Mary's Riding Centre

Carn Vean Café

Silvery Wave 1915

Vineyard

Holy Vale

A3110

Mount Todden Farm

Cairn

Battery

Mount Todden Down

Mount Todden Point

Longstone Holyvale footpath

Nature Trail

Darrity's Hole

Gap Point

Longstone Farm

ongstone

Water pumping

Normandy Farm

Desal Plant

Normandy House Community

Entrance

Normandy Down

Camper Cuttle

Deep Point

Long Rock menhir

Bant's Carn Battery

The big six-inch guns in the Garrison batteries could deal with a threat from large battleships at sea, but there were concerns at the start of World War II that St Mary's Harbour might be vulnerable to attack from small, fast-moving torpedo boats. This small battery, sited on the water's edge, was the response, although, by the time it was completed, the threat had passed and it was never armed. It's one of a pair; the other is the smaller Steval Battery on the Garrison. The building is private.

Telegraph and Long Rock menhir

Following the track up from Bar Point, a footpath leads off among the pine trees to this prehistoric standing stone or menhir. It's one of three good examples on Scilly; the other two are the Old Man of Gugh and the Mount Flagon menhir at Harry's Walls. They are usually thought to be among the oldest monuments in any landscape but because they often stand in isolation, their age can be difficult to pin down. However, Stone Age flint flakes were uncovered here in the 1920s.

Bant's Carn and Halangy Down Ancient Village

You might by now, after the tombs on Porth Hellick Down, Normandy Down and Innisidgen, be suffering from entrance grave fatigue, or possibly some form of prehistory ennui. Hold on for one last example, it's probably the best of all – Bant's Carn Tomb. Like other entrance graves, Bant's Carn Tomb was built about 4,000 years ago and, judging from the evidence of pottery fragments found inside, was in use for at least 500 years. Presumably, after that point the fashion for burial or cremation changed or, perhaps, different structures like cairns took over as the preferred focus of prehistoric ritual. It has two very well-preserved kerbs and, just like the Giant's Grave on Porth Hellick Down, a blocking or portal stone that restricts entry to the passage. Four cremations were found inside.

The original Bronze Age settlement, contemporary with the tomb, lay further down the hillside where Halangy Porth is now. The remains of hut walls, blackened fire hearths, discarded limpet shells

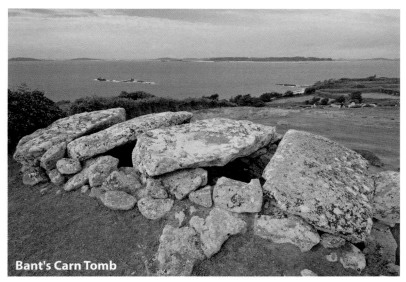
Bant's Carn Tomb

(a staple food on Scilly from prehistory to the 18th century) and pottery are slowly being eroded out of the cliff there. This first settlement seems to have been overwhelmed, not by the sea, but by drifting sand dunes in the Romano-British period 1,600 to 2,000 years ago. As a result the village was rebuilt a little further uphill, and closer to Bant's Carn Tomb which, even then, was 2,000 years old. It's the remains of this later Romano-British village that are visible today.

The tomb was originally sited on the uncultivated ground above the first settlement, the usual prehistoric pattern that can be seen on Samson, Northwethel and Gugh. But as the village was forced to move up-slope so the fields moved up with it and are clearly visible all around the tomb as stepped terraces. These terraces form over centuries as soil from ploughed fields is washed downhill to settle behind boundary walls. The same stepped terraces surround Lower Innisidgen Tomb, the earlier prehistoric fields there, and at Bar Point, having suffered the same inundation.

The new village included a courtyard house – a particularly West Cornish development in the Romano-British period. It uses the round hut design found everywhere on the islands (and under the sea) but adds workrooms placed around an enclosed courtyard. There's a similar example at the prehistoric settlement on Nornour in the Eastern Isles, and the layout echoes other courtyard house settlements in West Cornwall like the famous Chysauster and Carn Eûny villages near Penzance. Time now for a well-deserved crab sandwich and beer at Juliet's Garden.

2. St Agnes, Gugh, Annet and the Western Rocks

Kingdom of seals and seabirds

LONG BEFORE HUMANS ARRIVED ON SCILLY, St Agnes, Annet and the Western Rocks were a distinct group of islands all on their own, separated from the rest of Scilly by the deep water of St Mary's Sound. Anyone who's made the crossing from St Mary's to St Agnes when a northwesterly sea is running knows just how rough this stretch of water can be. So it's a psychological as well as a physical barrier, and the eighty residents of St Agnes and Gugh are a resilient and resourceful band.

Today, the only inhabited islands in this group are **St Agnes** and **Gugh**. Further west, the rocks and isles now belong exclusively to seals and seabirds, although in the past, humans have had a shaky and sporadic toehold here too. Hunters made seasonal camp on **Annet** in prehistory and in recent centuries divers have used **Rosevear** as a base for salvaging valuable cargo, as have blacksmiths working on the first Bishop Rock Lighthouse. Oddly, the place with the longest record of unbroken occupation in the Western Rocks is the **Bishop Rock**, perhaps the most remote, exposed and isolated place on Scilly. Lighthouse keepers lived here from 1858 to 1992 – surely Scilly's most perilous and lonesome address.

Of today's uninhabited isles, **Annet** and **Rosevear** are large enough to support a few species of maritime plants like thrift, sea beet and tree mallow. Others, like **Crebawethan** and **Melledgan**, are little more than bare rock, ground down to low stumps by the continual pounding of the waves. In a calm sea, they can be awash; with a strong sea running, waves roll right over them or crash into the rock faces sending up plumes of spray visible from miles away. At times like this, it's all the more magnificent to see the **Bishop Rock Lighthouse** standing bolt upright on the horizon. It's a reassuring presence, especially at night, as the beam from its lantern sweeps across the underside of the clouds.

ANNET/WESTERN RKS

Boats don't land here but sightseeing trips do come in close to watch the seals and birds. If the sea is calm enough, boats will continue to the Bishop Rock Lighthouse.

Perconger Quay

ST AGNES AND GUGH

All ferries land and leave from **Perconger Quay**. Boats run to St Mary's at least twice a day in the season. Trips to other off-islands and sightseeing trips run once or twice each week. Ferries from St Agnes are operated by **St Agnes Boating**.

FOOD AND DRINK
St Agnes Stores has picnic essentials. **Covean** and **Coastguards** are the two main cafes on St Agnes. The **Turk's Head** pub does pasties and sit down meals. **Troy Town Farm** makes its own ice-cream and dairy products.

BEACHES
Covean is a sheltered sun trap on even the blowiest of days, as is **Dropnose Porth** on Gugh. **The Bar** is good for families. **Periglis** is more open with views to the Bishop Rock Lighthouse and the Western Rocks.

Bishop Rock Lighthouse

To many of us, the ocean can seem an irredeemably hostile place and a boat trip to the Bishop is probably as far as we will ever venture. But for some Scillonian visitors – pelagic birds like shearwaters, storm petrels and puffins – the open sea is their home and it's on dry land where they look out of place. These birds would spend their whole lives on the ocean if they didn't have to make brief landfall on **Annet** and the **Western Rocks** to lay eggs and raise chicks. On land they have the comic ungainliness of a scuba diver walking on a quayside. Manx shearwaters are so unaccustomed to solid ground that their landing technique is simply to crash with a thump into the tussocks of thrift on Annet. It's a breathtaking contrast to see just how at home and how graceful they are on the ocean, skimming and shearing over the waves.

The **Western Rocks** have been responsible for hundreds of shipwrecks and the loss of thousands of lives. In the days of sail, a vessel was largely helpless in the face of a storm, driven relentlessly onwards to shatter, often in seconds, on the rocks. Their very names – **Hellweathers**, **Roaring Ledge**, **Tearing Ledge** – tell you all you need to know about the ferocity of the sea here. Sometimes the only clue that a wreck had even happened was a raft of flotsam arriving on the beaches of St Agnes, a tide of splintered wood, regurgitated cargo and bruised corpses, often stripped naked by the sea. Occasionally, survivors would make it to a nearby rock but might have to wait days for the seas to subside before they could be rescued. More often, no-one survived. The identity of a wreck could sometimes be inferred from the cargo it spilled into the sea – indigo, rum and cotton from the Caribbean; jute from Bengal; spices, coffee and tobacco from the Dutch East Indies. On several occasions islanders have woken to find the bays of St Agnes and Gugh brimful with produce, rafts of bobbing Valencia oranges or a sea of wheat. Any cargo too heavy to be taken by the tide would rain down on the rocky gullies from the disintegrating wreck above – silver dollars from the Spanish Main, African gold, bronze cannons and iron shot.

St Agnes
Scilly's original off-island

Covean

Surprisingly, the island is not named after a Christian saint at all; the name Agnes* comes from the Cornish *ek* for *beyond* or *far-off* and *enys* for *island*. This is the original Scillonian off-island. It's been separate for far longer than any of the other inhabited islands which, until about 500 years ago, were all connected to one another by sand dunes and salt marsh. It feels like it's been separate for a long time too, because even though it's the smallest of all the off-islands, it's absolutely full of personality and places. There are strange and wonderful rocks like the **Nag's Head** and the **Devil's Punch Bowl**, majestic carns that erupt out from the turf on **Castella** and **Wingletang Down** and, like every good storybook island, it's got a lighthouse too. There's an intimacy here, not just to do with its size, but to do with the place-names as well. Who was Grandfather Hugh and why does Uncle Tom have a quay named after him? Who was the boy found drowned on Boy's Rock? It's a place full of stories, somewhere to set your imagination running.

The Bar and Covean

St Agnes is an island of beaches, not the huge long beaches of Tresco and St Martin's, but more of secluded and secretive coves. Children particularly love playing on the sand bar at Perconger and watching excitedly as the tide creeps ever higher until it overtops the bar (but beware the dangerous currents when it's covered). Covean is the most secluded of beaches, a sun trap on the blowiest of days and perfect for exploring the foreshore at low water.

---

*   *The prefix 'saint' is a later addition and is frequently dropped by locals*

St Warna's Well

Wingletang and Beady Pool

Most of the paths on the north of Wingletang Down lead to the huge bun-shaped rock called the Devil's Punch Bowl (it has a basin on the very top). These large, oddly shaped rocks take on celebrity status in granite landscapes. There's almost always someone just standing here staring at the rock and you will probably find yourself doing exactly the same thing. Further down at Beady Pool, ceramic beads from a 17th century Dutch ship are sometimes found between the boulders around the high tide mark. They are about the size of a pea with a black glassy inside and a brown ceramic outside; others have black and white stripes. They are quite rare now, but after many years searching and collecting, people have managed to gather enough to string a necklace. Boy's Rock marks the place a child's body was recovered, possibly from the same wreck.

Ceramic beads from Beady Pool

St Warna's Well

Scilly has surprisingly few folk myths compared to West Cornwall and this has been cited as evidence that the off-islands may well have been abandoned altogether by humans for long periods in the past. However, in St Warna's Well, we have a fascinating survival of folk myth, certainly early Christian and possibly prehistoric. You might not guess it from the scant remains of the well itself – little more than a stone-lined pit with a few rough stone steps – but this is one of the most intriguing corners of Scilly. At least as far back as the Iron Age (700BC – AD400), springs were sacred places, believed to be conduits to and from the underworld. When Christianity arrived in the 6th century, these long-venerated Celtic sites were appropriated as Christian holy wells. Here we have St Awarna's holy well. We know nothing of Awarna herself and it's quite possible that, like Elidius and Theona on St Helen's and Teän, she was one of the many Celtic saints who arrived in Cornwall in the 6th and 7th centuries AD. That there is no record of her name elsewhere is not necessarily significant. These Celtic saints were often hermits, and after all we know nothing of Theona and very little about Elidius. What's particularly interesting

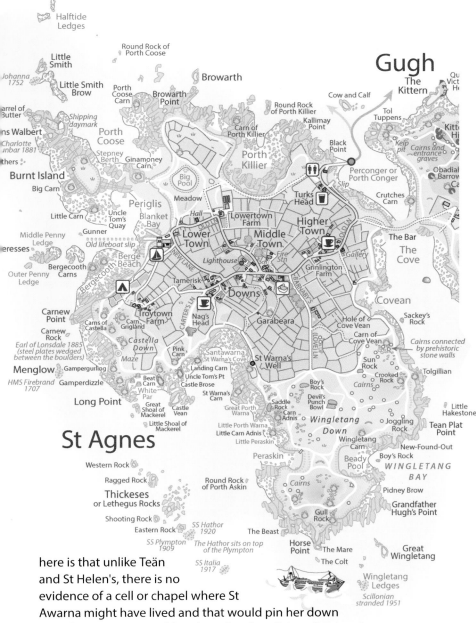

here is that unlike Teän and St Helen's, there is no evidence of a cell or chapel where St Awarna might have lived and that would pin her down to a Christian origin. Add to that a local tradition, dismissed for many years, that offerings thrown into the well would ease the passage of a ship onto the rocks (hardly a Christian invocation) and the beguiling thought grows that Awarna might actually be a memory from a pre-Christian period. She would certainly fit as one of the savage and vengeful water goddesses of Celtic religion. When the site was excavated in the 19th century several ancient gold pins were said to have been found at the bottom of the well.

The Nag's Head

St Agnes Lighthouse
This is one of Britain's earliest lighthouses, built in 1680 at a time when sea trade was growing rapidly and when the Western Rocks were culling large numbers of passing ships. Despite its impressive size, it was really too distant from the Western Rocks to be a great help and, as it could only display a weak light from a coal burning cresset, was all but useless in bad weather and fog. It was superseded in 1911 by Peninnis Head Lighthouse on St Mary's. It's not open to the public.

The Nag's Head, Castella Down, Troy Town Maze
It's difficult to believe that the Nag's Head is not man-made, so clearly does it resemble a horse's head, but like the Loaded Camel and numerous other Scillonian rocks, it is completely natural. The carns on Castella Down are particularly spectacular. They make a dramatic backdrop for Troy Town maze, said to have been constructed by a lighthouse keeper in the 19th century. Some think it may be older as similar mazes are found in Scandinavia and we know the Vikings certainly landed on Scilly.

Periglis – the last beach in the world
This really does feel like the last beach in the world with just the Western Rocks, the Bishop Rock Lighthouse and two thousand miles of ocean for company. The tiny white flakes of mica on the beach stick to your skin like fish scales so that children playing in the sand take on the appearance of mermaids or sea creatures – an appropriately Celtic transformation on this island of animalistic wind-sculpted rocks that come alive in the swirling sea mists. Along with Cruther's Hill and Samson Hill, the view southwest from here over the Western Rocks to the Bishop Rock is one of *the* views on Scilly. It certainly can send a shiver down your spine – part apprehension, part exhilaration – there's no mistaking you're on the very edge of the world.

The coal burning cresset used in St Agnes Lighthouse – now in Tresco Abbey Gardens

Gugh
Samson's little brother

Looking over The Bar to Gugh

Gugh (pronounced *goo*) is linked to St Agnes by a sand and shingle bar, so at least for a few hours each day, when the bar is covered, it can claim to be the smallest inhabited island on Scilly with a population in single figures. Check the tide times when you set off because the bar is covered for at least an hour either side of high water and strong currents make it unsafe to wade or swim back when it's covered. Your boatman will let you know the precise timings. The barns were constructed in the 1940s. Before that Gugh had probably been uninhabited since prehistory. The island forms the southern end of a chain of impressive and distinctive hills on the western edge of Scilly from Samson Hill on Bryher, passing through Samson itself, to here (Gugh is Cornish: *ughel* for *high place*). All have alignments of entrance graves on their summits – a sort of Beverly Hills of the prehistoric dead. Like Samson, Gugh has that pleasing, and very Scillonian, arrangement of twin hills joined by a low-lying neck.

Gugh's southern tip – Carn of Works and Dropnose Porth

The sunny southern end of Gugh is a particularly pleasant place to stop and enjoy the views out to sea. The area inland of the coast path and immediately around Carn of Works is closed when the gulls are raising chicks. The adult gulls will dive bomb you if you get too close and have an uncanny accuracy with their fishy faeces that discourages most intruders. The 'works' in Carn of Works refers to a Civil War gun platform (as it does on Bryher) that defended this side of St Mary's Sound. Dropnose Porth and Dropnose Rock (like an elephant's head and trunk) are similar to the rocks at Peninnis Point on St Mary's.

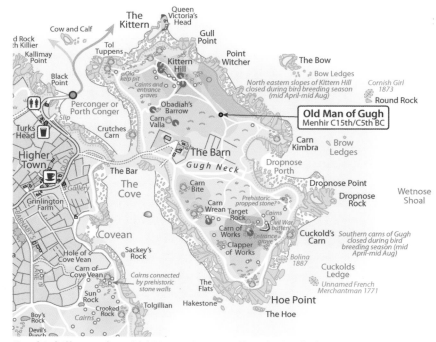

Gugh's hilly north – Old Man, Kittern Hill and Obadiah's Barrow

The Old Man of Gugh has been patiently standing here for the past 3,000 years. Compared to West Cornwall, Scilly has relatively few standing stones, possibly because by the time Scilly was settled in the later Bronze Age this type of monument had gone out of fashion. By contrast, the entrance grave was a fashion that lasted much longer on Scilly than on the mainland, and there are almost as many examples on Gugh as there are in the whole of Cornwall. As well as these ritual monuments, the stone bases of circular domestic huts poke through the turf at Tol Tuppens and on the northeast side of Kittern Hill, though they are usually lost in a sea of bracken by the end of the summer. Field walls associated with these prehistoric settlements are clearest on the more southern of the twin summits on Kittern Hill, where they join up with entrance graves and cairns. The pair of entrance graves on the northern summit are particularly well preserved. On the southern summit they are joined by a slightly later prehistoric stone field wall which follows the line of the path down to Obadiah's barrow, another good example of an entrance grave. Obadiah Hicks was a local farmer. It's a slightly unusual setting on the mid-slope of the hill as most entrance graves sit on the crest of hills. The original entrance is at the higher end of the passage.

All boats land at **Perconger Quay**. Don't forget, Gugh is cut off from St Agnes at high water so you will need to plan your visit to Gugh to coincide with low tide. Visitors staying elsewhere on Scilly often combine a visit to St Agnes with a boat trip to view Annet, the Western Rocks and the Bishop Rock Lighthouse.

Dropnose Porth on Gugh

St Agnes

The obvious thing to do is to just follow the coast but, if you have the time, St Agnes has a pleasant interior too – Barnaby's Lane is lovely.

To follow the coast path from the quay, take the track past **The Turk's Head** (where you can order a pasty for later), then follow the road uphill to where it turns sharply. Take the little track down to The Bar and follow the coast path to **Covean** where you can swim. Just beyond Sackey's Rock you can turn off the coast path up to **Wingletang Down** with its characterful rocks like **Sun Rock** and the **Devil's Punch Bowl. St Warna's Well** is easily missed – it's on the coast path but tucked under

a granite carn. For a cup of tea, follow the path inland from **Santawarna** (St Warna's Cove) up to **Coastguards** past the **Nag's Head**. Continuing on the coast path, **Castella Down** has impressive carns that erupt out of the turf. At **White Par** you can add to the piles of stones on the beach and pace around **Troy Town Maze**. The coast path is a little tricky along **Bergecooth** as it follows the top of the boulder beach – it's easier to follow the track through the campsite to the church at **Periglis**.

Distance
5.7km (3½ miles) following the coast.
Best picnic spots
Covean, Peraskin/Beady Pool, Periglis.

Gugh

It takes a little over an hour to stroll around the whole of Gugh (without dallying).

After crossing **The Bar** most people turn south and follow the coast path below **Carn Wrean** to **Hoe Point**. The section of sunny coastline to **Dropnose Point** is a good place to stop and sit. Swimmers will enjoy a dip at **Dropnose Porth**, which like Covean, is a secretive sheltered spot – arguably the two best beaches on Scilly. From here you can return to The Bar over Gugh Neck or continue up to **The Old Man** and then to **Kittern Hill** with its twin summits. If you can see your ferry coming into view around the Garrison, you'll probably want to shortcut from the south summit by following the path and prehistoric field wall down to **Obadiah's Barrow**. From the northern summit of Kittern Hill the path drops down to **Tol Tuppens** and follows the low cliff and coast back to The Bar.

Distance
3.5km (2¼ miles) from Perconger Quay.
Best picnic spots
Dropnose Porth or around Cuckold's Carn.

Troy Town Maze

Annet and Hellweathers
A fleeting landfall

Annet is Scilly's bird island. A low-lying, spray-washed isle, it looks featureless from a distance, but seen close up from a boat, **Carn Irish** and **The Haycocks** are two of the most impressive headlands on Scilly. Sea birds breed on many of the smaller islands but **Annet**, because of its size, is especially important. It's home in spring and early summer to breeding puffins and Manx shearwaters who burrow into the short turf. Storm petrels nest between the great boulders at the top of the beaches and herring, lesser black-backed and the ferocious but magnificent great black-backed gulls jostle for space between tussocks of thrift and on the cliff ledges.

Smaller birds like puffins, Manx shearwaters and storm petrels tend to spend the day at sea, keeping well out the way of the aggressive gulls who would otherwise prey on them. The best chance to see these attractive smaller birds is on one of the popular evening boat trips when the birds gather offshore, waiting for the safety of darkness before they return to their chicks. Puffins are a slightly odd mix of characteristics with a colourful clown bill and a comic waddling gait on dry land, sometimes even tumbling over their own oversize feet. In the air, their barrel shape makes them fast flyers but they lack the soaring grace of a gull. It's underwater where they come into their own, their small powerful wings and webbed feet allowing them to chase and catch small fish.

The *Thomas W Lawson* is lost
A steel-hulled, seven-masted schooner built to carry 11,000 tons of cargo, the *Thomas W Lawson* was one of the largest and strangest-looking sailing ships ever built – a supercarrier of her day. She set sail from America on 19th November 1907 and endured a stormy passage across the Atlantic losing most of her sails along the way. The Bishop Rock Lighthouse was sighted on 13th December but she was blown before the gale towards Annet. The captain let out his anchors in an attempt to hold his position but refused the offer to take to the St Agnes and St Mary's lifeboats – who had both stood by. The ship's cables lasted into the early hours of the next day but as the storm increased they parted one after another. She struck Shag Rock off Annet, the heavy seas lifting her onto the reef where she capsized. There were just two survivors; the rest of the crew were drowned and are buried in the graveyard of St Agnes Church.

Shark's Fin
Ruddy

Flat Ledge

York
1822

The
Haycocks

Annet
Head

Lake
Anthown

North
East
Porth

Butterman's
Point

SMITH SOUND

North
West
Porth

Minmanueth

Carn Irish

Thomas W Lawson
1907

Shag
Rock

West
Porth

Carn
Windlass

Annet Flats

Minmow

Outer
Ranneys

Moco
Rock

Smith's
Carn

Hollandia
1743

Middle
Ranneys

Inner
Ranneys

Annet
(Closed to visitors all year)

Landing
Beach

ANNET NECK

South
Carn

Hannah Louisa
1839

Flat Ledge

Old Woman's
House

Black
Rock

Hellweathers

Financier
1783

Shag
Rock

Menrounds

Custom
House
Rock

Providencia
1821

West
Carn

Peaked
Rock

Brow of
Hellweathers

HELLWEATHERS NECK

South
Carn

Storm petrel

Watty's
Rock

Hale
Rock

SHOAL NECK

The *Hollandia* is lost
The *Hollandia* belonged to
the Dutch East India Company
and was driven onto the west
coast of Annet with the loss
of 276 lives in June 1743. She
was loaded with Spanish
silver pieces-of-eight minted
in central America and was on
her maiden voyage to Dutch
Indonesia. More than 50,000
coins have been recovered
since the position of the
wreck was identified in the
early 1970s.

River Lune
1879

Flat Rock

Brothers

Isinvrank

MUNCOY NECK

Muncoy

Little
Menbean

Muncoy
Ledges

Great
Menbean

Seal
Rock

Menfleming

Flat
Carn

Melledgan
(Closed all year)

Doctor's Hole

Melledgan
Head

Great
Stone

Unnamed Dutch
merchantman 1760

Little
Stone

Biggal (child)
of Melledgan

The Western Rocks
A huge gaping maw

These are some of the most notorious reefs on the Western Approaches. Known over the centuries as the Dogs of Scilly, they have twice claimed more than 1,500 souls in a single night – once when the British Fleet foundered here in 1707, and once when three French Men O'War were wrecked near St Agnes in 1781. It's little wonder that the screams of seagulls here are said to mock the cries of drowning sailors. The Western Rocks consist of two parallel lines running roughly northwest to southeast. The outer line is quite permeable, stretching from the Crim Rocks through the Bishop to the Crebinicks. Directly at right angles to this is one of Scilly's main navigation channels, the Southwest Passage, which runs right beneath the Bishop Rock Lighthouse. It's so close that ships would sometimes stop and chat with the lighthouse keepers, although the prospect of having to sail so close to the Western Rocks must have filled a seaman with apprehension, a little like tiptoeing through a graveyard at night. A second inner line of rocks forms a much more impermeable barrier, an almost continuous crescent of low-lying ledges running from The Gilstone and Pednathise Head to Great Crebawethan – a huge gaping maw waiting to swallow any ship that ventures too close. If by some miracle a storm-bound ship managed to make its way through narrow gaps like Santasperry Neck, it might limp on to be finally impaled on Hellweathers or Annet. Once the Western Rocks got their teeth into their prey they rarely let it escape.

Admiral Shovell and the loss of the British Fleet 1707

Admiral Sir Cloudesley Shovell (1650–1707) was one of the most celebrated sailors of his time, a heroic figure and member of parliament. At the age of fifteen, during the Second Anglo-Dutch War of 1665 to 1667, he showed the sort of bravery that was later to become legendary by swimming between ships in the midst of battle with battle orders in his mouth. He had a long and distinguished service, firstly in the struggle with the Dutch Empire and then against the French and pirates threatening trade routes. In October 1707, the British fleet under Sir Cloudesley's command was returning from the Mediterranean with a fleet of twenty-one ships when they hit bad weather in the Bay of Biscay and became disorientated. Shovell called a meeting on his flagship, *HMS Association*, to try to reach agreement on their position. This decision was made more difficult by a long-standing error in nautical charts that showed Scilly ten miles further north before 1750 and compounded by the action of a poorly understood sea current that pushed ships further north than they expected. After much discussion, the consensus was that they were well south of Scilly. One captain did dissent. He was a Scillonian by birth and said that he thought them to be only a few miles west of the islands. Later that night the fleet struck the Western Rocks. Four ships went down in quick succession, *HMS Association* and *HMS Firebrand* on the Outer Gilstone, *HMS Eagle* on the Crim and *HMS Romney* on the Crebinicks. The next day, Sir Cloudesley's body was washed ashore, barely alive, at Porth Hellick on St Mary's where he was said to have been murdered by a local woman for his emerald ring. His body was buried at the head of the beach. It was later exhumed, pickled in brandy and laid to rest in Westminster Abbey.

The Longitude Prize

The loss of the British Fleet in 1707 highlighted once again the dangers of not being able to fix an accurate position at sea. A ship could establish its position along a north–south line, its latitude, by reference to the pole star in its constant position overhead. What it couldn't do with any accuracy was establish its position on an east–west line, its longitude. If cloud obscured the stars, the captain had no choice but to dead reckon, essentially making an informed guess of his position based on assumed speed and direction. The shock of the 1707 disaster spurred the Admiralty to set a prize for the first person to find a reliable method of establishing longitude. In theory this was straightforward; if you knew the time of midday at your departure point, you could measure the disparity between that and the time of midday at your present position. The number of hours, minutes and seconds could be translated into miles east or west of your starting point. In combination with your latitude this gave an exact position. If the theory was straightforward, the practice was anything but.

Accurate pendulum clocks were available on land but they could not keep time on a ship that was pitching and rolling on the ocean. One man started to work towards a solution. He was John Harrison, the son of a Yorkshire carpenter and a master clock maker. He spent the rest of his life working on a spring-based mechanism that would be unaffected by the motion of a ship. This became known as Harrison's Chronometer and was the forerunner of the pocket watch. Harrison eventually won the prize after a number of sea trials proved the accuracy of his chronometer. The full story is told in Dava Sobel's popular book *Longitude*.

Spanish pieces-of-eight

Gloria
1875

Thornliebank
1913

**Zantman's
Rock**

Susanna
1913

Crim Rocks

The Crim Rocks lie two
kilometres north-northwest of
the Bishop Rock Lighthouse

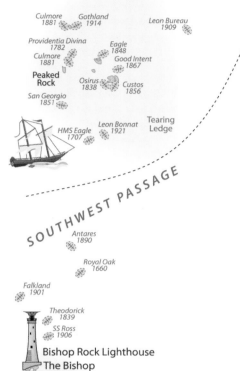

Culmore
1881

Gothland
1914

Leon Bureau
1909

Providentia Divina
1782

Eagle
1848

Culmore
1881

Good Intent
1867

**Peaked
Rock**

Osirus
1838

Custos
1856

San Georgio
1851

HMS Eagle
1707

Leon Bonnat
1921

Tearing
Ledge

Round Rock of
Crebawethan

Douro
1843

Nyanza
1898

Amel
181

Condor's Rocks

Phoenix
1680

**Great
Crebawethan**

SOUTHWEST PASSAGE

Zeelilie
1795

Unnamed
Venetian
Merchantman
1780

**Little
Crebawethan**

Antares
1890

Sprowse's
Brow

Pownall
1759

Minerva
1836

Royal Oak
1660

SS Castleford
1887

Wee

Falkland
1901

CREBAWETHAN NE

Cornish
Ledge

Theodorick
1839

SS Ross
1906

Bishop Rock Lighthouse

The Bishop

Western Rock
or
The Dogs of Scilly

Supply
1617

The Clerk

Tearing Ledge
Belinda
1854

HMS Romney
1707 Flat Ledge

Retarrier Ledges

SS Schiller
1875

Crebinicks

U681
1944

Grey seal

50

The loss of the *Schiller* in 1875

The *Schiller*, an early transatlantic liner, was on route from New York to Plymouth when, on the evening of 7th May 1875, she ran into thick fog just off Scilly. Knowing that he was near the islands, the captain ordered the engines to dead slow and edged forward with passengers helping to keep a look out for the Bishop Rock light. She must have passed close by without realising it, and struck without warning on the Retarrier Ledges. The captain managed to reverse off but the ship was then twisted broadside by a series of large waves that crushed most of the lifeboats on the exposed side and, as the ship listed over, made it impossible to launch the lifeboats on the other side too. Panic followed and the captain used his gun to restore order, but in the end only two lifeboats were successfully launched. The remaining passengers and crew took refuge in the deck house, hoping they would be safe there until daybreak brought help. However, the deck house was flattened by a huge wave taking with it many of the surviving passengers and crew. Of the 372 passengers and crew only 37 survived. A few did so by clinging to the rigging through the night; the rest somehow made it to the safety of Rosevean and Rosevear. The ship now lies in the boulders and gullies to the west of Retarrier Ledges, a mass of plates and spars flattened by the sea. Although it was heavily salvaged soon after its loss, persistent rumours of gold and silver bullion strewn across the reef still draw divers today.

lier
16

Brow of the ponds

Aurora
1860

Jacky's Rock

THE PONDS

olly Rock

Thames
1841

Sado
1870

Prinses Maria
1686

Silver Carn

Europe
1925

Cite de Verdun
1925

SANTASPERRY NECK

Frenchman's Rock

Biggal (or child)
of Gorregan

Blacksmith used during
the construction of the
first Bishop Rock
Lighthouse

Rosevear

Catherine
1807

Nancy
1784

ROSEVEAR NECK

Rosevear
Ledges

Smyrna
1752

Enfant de Bretagne
1977

Rosevean

ROSEVEAN NECK

Dry Splat

Vink

Daisy

Black Rock

Inner
Rags

Rags

SHOAL NECK

BROAD NECK

Gorregan

Carn
Lawrance

Carn
Captain

Hole of Gorregan

Camperdown

Trenemene

Mary
1788

HMS Association and
HMS Firebrand 1707

Outer Gilstone
Ledges

Outer
Istone

Old
Bess

Pednathise Head

SS Antonios
1912

51

The Bishop Rock Lighthouse
The loneliest address on Scilly

The Bishop Rock has been performing the last rites on ships and crews ever since man first set sail in this part of the world. Why it's called the Bishop is not clear. It's said that before the lighthouse was built, the shape of the rock resembled a bishop's mitre; others say that it, and its near neighbour, the Clerk, are named after two men found clinging there after a wreck in the 17th century. There's no dispute though that, along with the Wolf Rock*, this is one of the most exposed lighthouses in Britain. It's completely open to the Atlantic and vulnerable to very large waves that pile up to a great height as the seabed beneath them abruptly shallows.

The first attempt to mark the Western Rocks, and one of the first lighthouses in Britain, was built on St Agnes in 1680. But as it's seven kilometres from the Bishop, and only had a weak light from a coal burning cresset (now in Tresco Abbey Gardens), it was all but useless in bad weather and fog. A more effective beacon was required. For many years the task of building a lighthouse in such an exposed location proved too great, but in 1847, plans were eventually agreed for a lighthouse with cast iron columns anchored to the rock with huge, half-metre long bolts. It was hoped that the open structure would allow waves to pass through without causing damage.

A blacksmith shop and accommodation was set up on Rosevear in 1847 (the buildings are still standing). It took three years to construct, work being suspended each winter and resumed in the following spring. It was hard work but lightened on one occasion by an evening masked ball. By the beginning of 1850, the lighthouse was nearing completion but on the night of 5th February, just a few weeks before it was to be officially commissioned, the lighthouse was washed from its base. It took one storm, one night, to undo three years' work. Prospective lighthouse keepers could have been forgiven for being rather apprehensive at the thought of serving on the Bishop.

Work started in 1852 on a replacement, this time using a solid tower constructed from carefully dovetailed blocks of Cornish granite – a design pioneered for the third Eddystone lighthouse in 1759. It saved lives even before it was completed in September 1858 when survivors of a wreck were found sheltering in the partially completed structure by a group of surprised masons. Unfortunately it soon became apparent that it too was not strong enough to totally resist the very large waves to which the Bishop is subjected. Thin cracks started snaking up the sides of the tower and vibrations, caused by the

---

* *The Wolf Rock Lighthouse lies about 30km due east of Scilly, 15km south-southwest of Land's End and is clearly visible to the south from the Scillonian and when flying to Scilly or the mainland.*

waves passing over the lighthouse, made it shake violently, knocking plates off the shelves. A keeper once saw a fish swim past the kitchen window twenty-five metres up, as a wave passed over the lighthouse. In April 1874 waves of forty metres broke clear over the tower, washing away the lantern and bringing tons of water into the lighthouse, threatening to drown the keepers inside. In 1882 it was decided to construct an outer skin of stone around the existing tower – increasing both its height and strength. Since then the structure has been without problems. The last keeper left in 1992 when the lighthouse became fully automated, ending 134 years of continuous occupation.

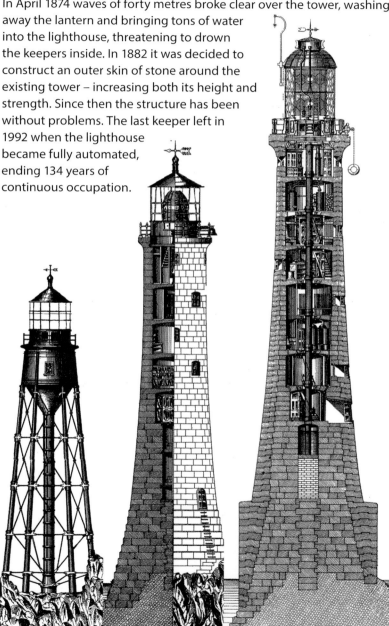

The first lighthouse was washed away before it was even commissioned.

The second lighthouse was more successful, but cracks soon started to snake up the sides.

The third lighthouse encased the second.

Entrance grave on the summit of South Hill on Samson – looking north to Bryher and the Norrard Rocks

3. Bryher, Samson and the Norrard Rocks

Rough-hewn western hills

MORE THAN ANY OTHER ISLAND ON Scilly, **Bryher** has the feeling of being on a frontier, in a combat zone between sea and land. The battle is played out most dramatically on **Shipman Head Down** where, even on the sunniest of summer days, you can sense how unnervingly wild it is in poor weather. During storms, waves crash into **Hell Bay** sending clouds of spray cascading right over the island to land in New Grimsby Sound: not a time to find yourself standing anywhere near **Badplace Hill**. Further south on Bryher, the coast is a little more sheltered, and around **Popplestones**, **Great Par** and **Rushy Bay** the coastal scenery is the most beautiful in Scilly, a perfect balance of bay, beach and carn-topped hill.

All the Scillonian off-islands have had periods where they've been abandoned completely by humans. **Samson** is the most recent example, its ruined houses lending it a wistful air, a reminder of the makeshift nature of living on the western margin of Scilly. It's a hugely attractive island and one of those places that roots itself deep in the memory so that when you recollect a visit, even many years later, you're drawn back with a startling intensity to the carns, the tombs and the sparkling sea.

The **Norrard** or **Northern Rocks** sit a little higher in the water than their counterparts the Western Rocks but, like them, they support little life beyond the short visits of breeding sea birds. All that changes though when you glance over the side of the boat. The **Garden of the Maiden Bower** may sound like an English cottage garden full of roses and apple blossom, but really it's a garden of seaweeds, full of tangle, furbellows, cuvie and the hypnotic waving fronds of dabberlocks. If you're lucky, you'll glimpse a shadow slipping and sliding between the watery sunbeams, because the only maidens that live here are mermaids and seals.

SAMSON
There are daily landings in the summer (tides permitting). Samson has no shops so remember to bring a picnic, sun cream and water.

The Bar, Bryher

NORRARD ROCKS
Boat trips run most days in the summer but don't land. You can jump off on Bryher or Tresco for lunch and sightseeing.

BRYHER
Ferries land at **Church Quay** at high water and at **The Bar** (Anneka's Quay) at low water. On extreme low tides, landing is at **Rushy Bay**. Visitors from St Mary's can land on Bryher in the morning, hop over to Tresco on the lunchtime boat and return from Tresco in the late afternoon (usually from Carn Near). If you're staying on Bryher, the ferries are run by Tresco Boat Services.

FOOD AND DRINK
Bryher Stores, **Vine Cafe**, **Fraggle Rock Bar** and **Hell Bay Hotel**.

BEACHES
Church Quay Beach is popular with families, **Rushy Bay** is a favourite for many, **Great Par** for late afternoon sun.

Rush hour traffic gathers
at The Bar on Bryher

Bryher
An unmistakably Scillonian landscape

Watch Hill

The root of the name Bryher is in the Cornish word *brea* meaning
hill, and the island is a procession of prominent and elegant hills all
tethered to one another by low-lying necks and sandy bars. It would
only need sea levels to rise by a few metres for the southern part of
Bryher to transform itself into a group of five or six separate islands.
As all these hills – **Gweal**, **Timmy's**, **Watch**, **Heathy** and **Samson** – are
too exposed and windswept to be cultivated, Bryher's ninety residents
have to make their lives in a relatively narrow zone, compressed
between hill and shore. A few fields and houses inch up the hillsides
at **The Town** and **Norrard**, but even here the hills dominate, giving
Bryher an innately rough-hewn character closer to Samson and Gugh
than to the more cultivated demeanour of other inhabited islands.

The wild north – Shipman Head Down

The northern third of Bryher is, like Tresco, a substantial plateau of
high ground, as rocky, exposed and dramatic as anywhere on Scilly.
It supports only a very thin, skeletal soil and everywhere the granite
bedrock breaks through so that only the hardiest maritime plants like
heather and English stonecrop grow here. Hardly any plants are more
than a few centimetres high and even they have to hug the ground
to avoid the salt winds that sweep across the island. Too exposed to
be useful to the living, Shipman Head Down is instead inhabited by
the prehistoric dead. The place is one huge prehistoric cemetery and
more than one hundred cairns sit on the surface. These low, man-
made mounds of stone and turf have been greatly eroded over the last
3,000 years and can be difficult to recognise, but the longer you look,

Great Par and Carn of Bars with Castle Bryher on the horizon

the more they stand out. Many are aligned on, or linked by, tumbled walls which are easier to spot. The exact role of cairns in prehistoric landscapes is unclear. Some are obviously part of prehistoric burials or cremation rituals but many contain no obvious artefacts or remains. Here, they clearly form part of a wider ritual landscape, a prehistoric cemetery in use for far longer than the graveyards of today's parish churches. The northern tip of the island is fortified with the earth and stone ramparts of Shipman Head Cliff Castle. Like the Giant's Castle on St Mary's, this is thought to date from the 1st and 2nd centuries AD and is assumed to be a refuge of last resort from marauding raiders.

The exposed western coast of Bryher

Hell Bay, Popplestones, Gweal Hill, Great Par and Heathy Hill

The waves that arrive in Hell Bay have often travelled for hundreds of kilometres so that when they are suddenly slowed by the rough seabed here, they build to a great height and hit the coast with a shuddering thud. Hell Bay then becomes a furious, confused cauldron of foam. It's one of the best places to be after a gale has blown through, when the skies have cleared but a strong sea is still running. South of Shipman Head Down the coast is much less exposed. Gweal and the Norrard Rocks take the sting out of the sea so that the coast softens and achieves a beautiful balance between sweeping bays like Popplestones and Great Par, and hilltops like Gweal Hill. Here are all the ingredients that make Scilly so attractive: curved bays filled with granite boulders, sandy beaches backed by dunes and every inlet guarded by a carn-topped hill. It's unmistakably Scillonian.

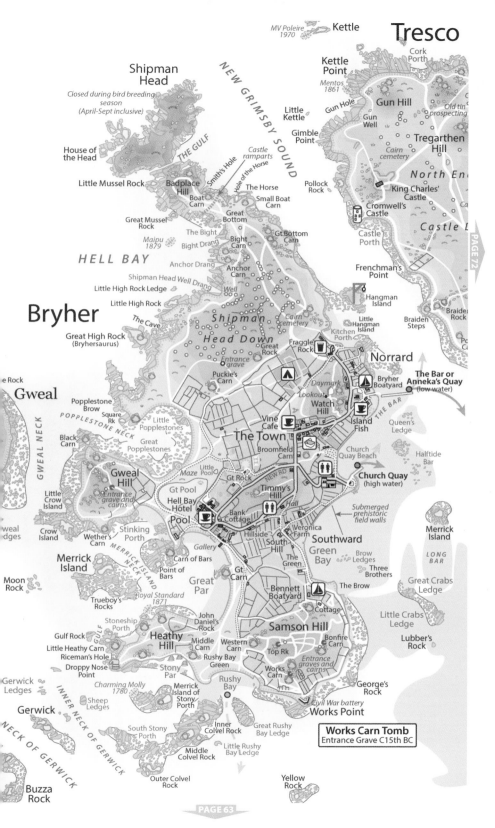

Tresco

MV Poleire
1970
Kettle

Cork
Porth

Kettle
Point

NEW GRIMSBY SOUND

Mentos
1861

Little
Kettle

Gun Hole

Gun Hill

Old tin
prospecting

Gun
Well

Gimble
Point

Tregarthen
Hill

North End

Shipman
Head

*Closed during bird breeding
season
(April-Sept inclusive)*

Castle
ramparts

Smith's Hole

Hole of the Horse

King Charles'
Castle

Cromwell's
Castle

THE GULF

House of
the Head

The Horse

Pollock
Rock

Little Mussel Rock

Badplace
Hill

Boat
Carn

Small Boat
Carn

Castle La

Great
Bottom

Great Mussel
Rock

The Bight

*Maipu
1879*

Gt.Bottom
Carn

Castle
Porth

Bight
Carn

Frenchman's
Point

HELL BAY

Anchor Drang

The Bight Drang

Bight Drang

Anchor
Carn

Hangman
Island

Braiden
Rock

Shipman Head Well Drang

Well

Little
Hangman
Island

Braiden
Steps

Little High Rock Ledge

Little High Rock

Cairn
cemetery

*Shipman
Head Down*

Kitchen
Porth

Port
Ca

Bryher

The Cave

Fraggle
Rock

Norrard

Great High Rock
(Bryhersaurus)

*Entrance
grave*

Great
Rock

**The Bar or
Anneka's Quay**
(low water)

Puckle's
Carn

Daymark
Lookout

Bryher
Boatyard

Gweal

Popplestone
Brow

Square
Rk

Watch
Hill

THE BAR

Little
Popplestones

Vine
Cafe

Island
Fish

Queen's
Ledge

GWEAL NECK

POPPLESTONE NECK

Black
Carn

Great
Popplestones

The Town

Broomfield
Carn

Church
Quay Beach

Halftide
Bar

Gweal
Hill

Maze

Little
Pool

Gt Rock

NEW RD

Church Quay
(high water)

Merrick
Island

*Entrance
grave and
cairns*

Gt Pool

Timmy's
Hill

Little
Crow
Island

Crow
Island

Wether's
Carn

Stinking
Porth

**Hell Bay
Hotel**

Pool

Bank
Cottage

Hall

LONG
BAR

Veronica
Farm

*Submerged
prehistoric
field walls*

weal
dges

MERRICK ISLAND NECK

Hillside

South
Hill

Southward

Merrick
Island

Moon
Rock

Gallery

Carn of Bars

**Green
Bay**

The Green

Brow
Ledges

Three
Brothers

Great Crabs
Ledge

**Merrick
Island**

Point of
Bars

Gt
Carn

**Great
Par**

Bennett
Boatyard

The Brow

Little Crabs
Ledge

Trueboy's
Rocks

*Royal Standard
1871*

John
Daniel's
Rock

Cottage

Lubber's
Rock

Stoneship
Porth

Middle
Carn

Western
Carn

Samson Hill

Bonfire
Carn

Gulf Rock

GULF

Little Heathy Carn

**Heathy
Hill**

Rushy Bay
Green

Top Rk

Riceman's Hole

Droppy Nose
Point

Stony
Par

*Charming Molly
1780*

Merrick
Island of Stony
Porth

*Entrance
graves and
cairns*

Works
Carn

George's
Rock

Works Point

Gerwick
Ledges

INNER NECK OF GERWICK

Sheep
Ledges

Rushy
Bay

Inner
Colvel Rock

Great Rushy
Bay Ledge

Civil War battery

Works Carn Tomb
Entrance Grave C15th BC

Gerwick

South Stony
Porth

Middle
Colvel Rock

Little Rushy
Bay Ledge

NECK OF GERWICK

**Buzza
Rock**

Outer Colvel
Rock

Yellow
Rock

PAGE 72

PAGE 63

Rushy Bay with Mincarlo in the background

The sheltered south and east coast of Bryher
Green Bay, Samson Hill and Rushy Bay

A line of large stones march across the foreshore and into the water at Green Bay – the remains of a 3,000-year-old prehistoric field wall. Presumably more walls lie between here and Tresco as both islands are joined at low water by huge areas of sand. On the lowest tides of the year, around the spring and autumn equinox, you can walk all the way from Green Bay to Crabs Ledge, Plumb Rocks and on to Tresco. The area around The Green and Veronica Farm is about the only place on the island that gets enough shelter for it to feel lush and green. It feels all the more luxuriant because Bryher's character is very much defined by its exposed hills and cliffs. Nearby at Bennett Boatyard, you can hire dinghies and kayaks to explore the little isles and rock ledges between Bryher and Tresco.

This southern part of Bryher is dominated by Samson Hill. There are panoramic views from its summit east over the calm turquoise waters to Tresco, south over Rushy Bay to Samson, and west to the Norrard Rocks. A fine entrance grave sits on a granite outcrop just below Works Carn (it can be a little difficult to get to in late summer). Lower down the hill and just above the shore at Works Point is a Civil War battery, now just a grassy flat platform; it's a perfect place to stop for a picnic. Rushy Bay is one of the most popular beaches on Scilly and the landing beach of last resort if the tides are particularly low and boats can't get to Church Quay or The Bar. It's named after the Marram grass that grows on the dunes here.

Ferries call at **Church Quay** or **The Bar** (Anneka's Quay). Both are in the middle of Bryher, so you can head north onto Shipman Head Down, or south to Samson Hill. A visit to Bryher can be combined with a boat trip to the Norrard Rocks or take a lunchtime ferry across to Tresco and return to St Mary's from Carn Near.

The view from Samson Hill to Church Quay and Tresco

Shipman Head Down

A walk on the wild side of Scilly. The northern end of Bryher is a high plateau, always too exposed to be cultivated. Instead it's covered with cairns – prehistoric ritual structures, some associated with burials and cremations.

From **Church Quay**, walk along the beach to **The Bar** or, follow the road to **The Town** where you can pick up provisions in **Bryher Stores** or stop at **Vine Cafe**. Continue to **Norrard**. Immediately in front of **Fraggle Rock Bar**, turn left up the farm track for 30m then turn right following a path up through the fields to the high ground (a path also crosses the beach at **Kitchen Porth** but is often overgrown beyond). Once on

the high ground of Shipman Head Down you are walking in a Bronze Age cemetery. The cairns are a little difficult to make out being constructed of turf that has eroded over the centuries – it's easier to follow the walls that connect them. Cross **Shipman Head Down** to **Badplace Hill** and to the ramparts of the cliff castle overlooking **Hell Bay**. To return, follow the coast path to **Popplestones** and, if you have time, climb **Gweal Hill** for the views. Refreshments available at Hell Bay Hotel.

Distance
About 5km (3 miles) from Church Quay to Badplace Hill, Gweal Hill, Pool and back.
Places to picnic and swim
Church Quay, Gweal Hill, Great Par.

Samson and Gweal hills

This is the softer side of Bryher. A wonderful mix of landscapes – sandy beach, rocky bays, hills and dunes. Samson Hill has great views back to Tresco and over to Samson and the Norrard Rocks.

From **Church Quay**, follow the path south to **Green Bay**. Either follow the coast path around the base of **Samson Hill** or, take the path up to **Bonfire Carn** and the summit with its fine views. **Rushy Bay** is one of the best beaches on Scilly. A little further on is **Heathy Hill**, a good place to stop and picnic, and at **Great Par** you have the chance to visit **Golden Eagle Studio** or to stop at the **Hell Bay Hotel** for refreshments. If you've got time, wander up to the top of **Gweal Hill** which has great views back over the bays of Bryher – it's especially beautiful in the evening. Return to **Church Quay** or **The Bar** to pick up your ferry.

Distance
About 4.6km (2¾ miles) from Church Quay to Southward, Works Point, Heathy Hill, Gweal Hill, Pool and back.
Places to picnic and swim
Swim at Church Quay Beach, Rushy Bay, Great Par. Picnic on Heathy or Gweal Hill.

Hiring kayaks at Green Bay

Samson
An island with a magical pull

Landing Beach on Samson

This small, now uninhabited island has an almost magical pull on visitors and is often the most vividly remembered part of any holiday on Scilly. It's the classic Scillonian island type, a neat figure-of-eight formed of twin hills connected by a narrow, low-lying waist. It's so shapely and well proportioned it looks as if someone has designed it or drawn it on a map to bring it into being – an impression confirmed by that other typically Scillonian trait of naming picturesque places with the most prosaic of names. Here we get **North** and **South Hill**, **East** and **West Par**, a terse and pithy description of the island's geography but one that does little justice to the beauty of the place.

The ruins of an early prehistoric settlement lie beneath the sands of East Par. Neolithic flints found here date the site to the centuries around 3000BC. So this may have been one of the pioneer camps on Scilly (like Old Quay on St Martin's) used first by nomadic Stone Age hunters and then, when agriculture reached the islands around 1500BC, by Bronze Age farmers. At this time Samson, along with Bryher, was part of a range of western hills on Scilly and a low-lying plain stretched across to Tresco. Prehistoric field walls from that time are easily picked out from the top of Samson as dark lines beneath the sea and as the tide falls are revealed as seaweed-covered boulders running across Samson Flats to Black Ledge. They are easy to follow across the sand and even today, on the lowest tides of the year, it's perfectly possible to walk across to Tresco and only get your knees wet (photo page 18). The same walls were used in the 19th century to catch fish trapped on the falling tide.

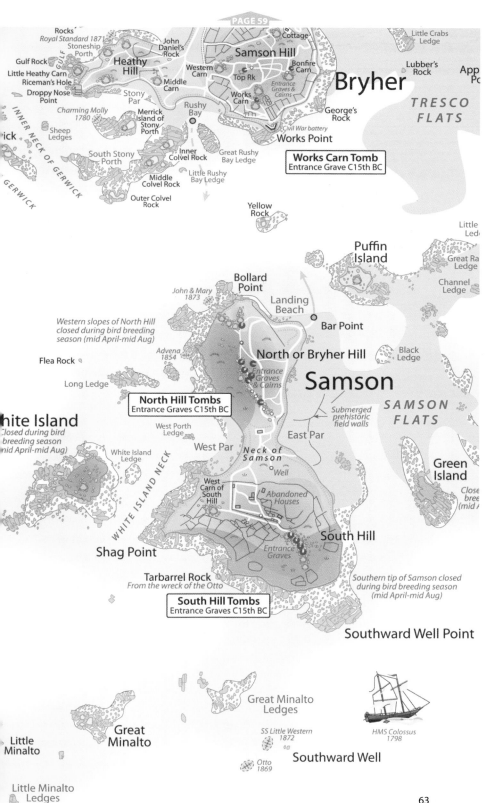

PAGE 59

Rocks
Royal Standard 1871
Stoneship
Gulf Rock · Porth
Little Heathy Carn
Riceman's Hole
Droppy Nose
Point

John
Daniel's
Rock

Cottage

Little Crabs
Ledge

**Heathy
Hill**

Western
Carn
Middle
Carn

*Charming Molly
1780*

Merrick
Island of
Stony
Porth

Sheep
Ledges

South Stony
Porth

Stony
Par

Rushy
Bay

Inner
Colvel Rock

Middle
Colvel Rock

Outer Colvel
Rock

Samson Hill

Top Rk

Works
Carn

*Entrance
Graves &
Cairns*

Bonfire
Carn

Bryher

Lubber's
Rock

George's
Rock

Civil War battery

Works Point

Great Rushy
Bay Ledge

Little Rushy
Bay Ledge

Yellow
Rock

**TRESCO
FLATS**

App
Po

Works Carn Tomb
Entrance Grave C15th BC

---

rick

INNER NECK OF GERWICK

GERWICK

*John & Mary
1873*

*Western slopes of North Hill
closed during bird breeding
season (mid April-mid Aug)*

Flea Rock

Long Ledge

hite Island

*losed during bird
breeding season
mid April-mid Aug)*

White Island
Ledge

Shag Point

WHITE ISLAND NECK

*Advena
1854*

West Porth
Ledge

West Par

West
Carn of
South
Hill

Tarbarrel Rock
From the wreck of the Otto

**Bollard
Point**

Landing
Beach

North or Bryher Hill

*Entrance
Graves
& Cairns*

Samson

*Neck of
Samson*

East Par

Well

*Submerged
prehistoric
field walls*

*Abandoned
Houses*

Bar Point

Black
Ledge

**Puffin
Island**

Little
Ledg

Great Ra
Ledge

Channel
Ledge

**SAMSON
FLATS**

Green
Island

Clos
bree
(mid A

South Hill

*Entrance
Graves*

North Hill Tombs
Entrance Graves C15th BC

South Hill Tombs
Entrance Graves C15th BC

*Southern tip of Samson closed
during bird breeding season
(mid April-mid Aug)*

Southward Well Point

**Little
Minalto**

**Great
Minalto**

Little Minalto
Ledges

**Great Minalto
Ledges**

*SS Little Western
1872*

*Otto
1869*

*HMS Colossus
1798*

Southward Well

Prehistoric field wall on Samson Flats

The name Samson comes from St Sampson, a 6th century Welsh saint. He's known to have travelled the sea between Wales, Cornwall and Brittany and is venerated at Golant near Fowey and on Guernsey. If he did stay here, he can't have stayed for long because he is most famous for founding the monastery at Dol de Bretagne where he died sometime around AD560. About thirty years ago a stone-lined grave was uncovered on the foreshore of East Par, possibly associated with the lost chapel of St Sampson. Subsequent excavations uncovered a timber structure from the 6th century AD and further north the foundations of a later, rectangular stone building, two graves and a rough stone font.

After a long period of being uninhabited, Samson was resettled, probably after the end of the English Civil War (1642–1651) so that by the beginning of the 19th century about forty people were living here. They seem to have lived in pretty dire circumstances, subsisting mostly on potatoes and limpets and what they could catch. Even today there are large waste tips of limpet shells outside the front door of every cottage (as there are outside many prehistoric huts). The island was really too small and its resources were too poor to comfortably support a community of that size. Water was difficult to collect and there was no wood for fuel so the islanders had to rely on collecting bracken and driftwood from the shore. In the early part of the 19th century the island was hit by a series of droughts, and by the time Augustus Smith took on the lease of the islands in 1834, most of the inhabitants were destitute. Alternative housing was provided for them on St Mary's and by 1855 the island was empty.

Part of Samson's attraction comes from the romantic allure of an island abandoned, with its roofless cottages, disued wells and tumbled field walls. The picturesque decay of the abandoned cottages was an inspiration for the poet Tennyson and for Sir Walter Besant who set the Victorian novel *Armorel of Lyonesse* here. Samson soon became a popular place to picnic. *Why the Whales Came* by Michael Morpurgo is partly set here and partly on Bryher.

Abandoned house on Samson

The loss of *HMS Colossus*

The *Colossus* spent the summer of 1798 hunting Napoleon's fleet in the
Mediterranean. She took part in the Battle of Cape St Vincent and also
in the Battle of the Nile in which Lord Nelson inflicted a decisive defeat
on the French navy. She was badly damaged in the encounters and
retired to Naples for repairs and celebrations; both were short lived.
Napoleon's army was approaching and Sir William Hamilton, the British
representative to the Court of Naples and husband of the famous Lady
Emma, was forced to evacuate to Palermo but not before his wife's
heart missed a beat on meeting Nelson. Although the *Colossus* was
in poor shape she was forced to make her way under escort to Scilly
where she anchored in St Mary's Sound in late November 1798. A
week of southerly gales keep her in Scilly and her already strained and
damaged fabric deteriorated further so that on 10th December, when
her main anchor cable parted and she was driven onto Southward
Well reef, she broke apart in minutes. The crew were saved by local
boats but the ship was a complete loss along with most of Sir William's
priceless second collection of Etruscan and Greek pottery (his first
makes up the core of the British Museum's collection). The
site was located in 1970 and fragments of Etruscan
pottery were recovered. In 2002 the beautifully carved
sternboard turned up on the seabed in an incredibly
good state of preservation. More information is available
on the Cornwall and Isles of Scilly Maritime Archaeology
Society (CISMAS) website.

The Norrard Rocks
A mermaid's garden

Of all the lovely place-names found on the Isles of Scilly,
The Garden of the Maiden Bower is probably the most beautiful,
but if any maidens ever did skip through here, they must have been
mer-maidens gliding around the forest of kelp just as the seals do
today. The sheltered boulder beach at the **Brow of Mincarlo** and
Illiswilgig are breeding sites for seals, and sightseeing trips come to
watch them bask here and on the flat rocks and boulders around
Seal Rock and **Scilly Rock**. The most distinctive profile in
the Norrard Rocks belongs to **Castle Bryher**. It looks like
Hanjague's twin and is easily the most recognisable
of all the Norrard Rocks. **Illiswilgig**, **Castle Bryher**
and **Mincarlo** are also home to breeding pairs
of guillemots, razorbills, puffins, cormorants
and gulls. All these rocks are streaked with
fishy guano, wafts of which catch in the
nostrils as the boat passes by. Only hardy
seashore specialists like sea beet, thrift
and the shingle-loving orache can deal
with the conditions here. In particular,
sea beet and orache seem to thrive on
the disturbance caused by the birds
and are able to tolerate the nitrate-rich
guano that washes down on them. In
some years trailing mats of Hottentot fig
appear, presumably from fragments of
plant transported here from the gardens of
Bryher by nest-building birds.

Wreck of the *SS Minnehaha*

The *Minnehaha* grounded on Scilly Rock on
18th April 1910 after becoming lost in thick fog
on her way from New York to Tilbury. The sea was
calm so the sixty-six passengers and a hold full of
cattle were ferried to safety without incident. In an
attempt to lighten the ship and float her off the rocks
before she became a total wreck, the captain ordered
all the cargo in the forward holds to be jettisoned
overboard. Crates of cigarettes, early American roadsters
and grand pianos drifted away from the stranded ship,
some to be towed ashore by islanders who are said to have
smoked themselves silly for the next year. She was eventually
pulled free on a spring tide in mid-May.

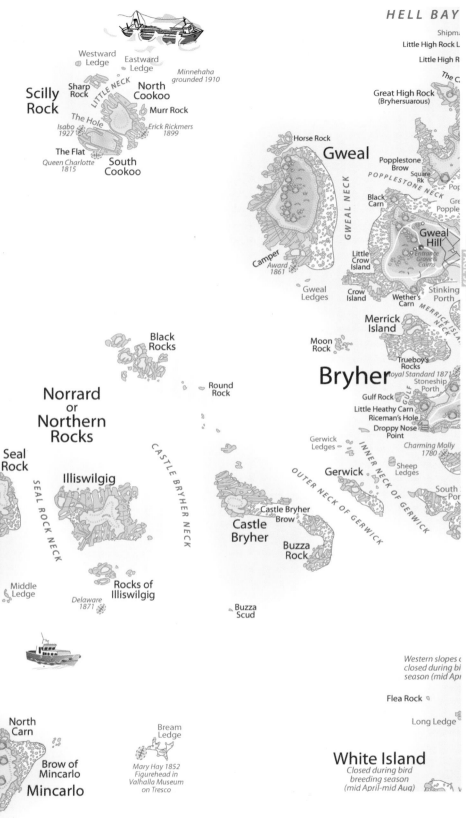

Shipma
Little High Rock L
Little High R

Westward
Ledge
Eastward
Ledge

Minnehaha
grounded 1910

The C

Sharp
Rock
North
Cookoo

Scilly
Rock

Great High Rock
(Bryhersuarous)

LITTLE NECK

Murr Rock

The Hole

Isabo
1927

Erick Rickmers
1899

Horse Rock

Gweal

Popplestone
Brow

Square
Rk

Pop

The Flat

Queen Charlotte
1815

South
Cookoo

POPPLESTONE NECK

Black
Carn

Gre
Popple

GWEAL NECK

Gweal
Hill

Entrance
Grave &
Cairns

Camper

Award
1861

Little
Crow
Island

Gweal
Ledges

Crow
Island

Wether's
Carn

Stinking
Porth

MERRICK ISLA

Black
Rocks

Moon
Rock

Merrick
Island

Round
Rock

Trueboy's
Rocks

Norrard
or
Northern
Rocks

Bryher

Royal Standard 1871

Stoneship
Porth

CASTLE BRYHER NECK

Gulf Rock

Little Heathy Carn

GULF

Seal
Rock

Illiswilgig

Riceman's Hole

Droppy Nose
Point

SEAL ROCK NECK

Gerwick
Ledges

Charming Molly
1780

Sheep
Ledges

INNER NECK OF GERWICK

Gerwick

South
Po

OUTER NECK OF GERWICK

Castle Bryher
Brow

Castle
Bryher

Buzza
Rock

Middle
Ledge

Rocks of
Illiswilgig

Delaware
1871

Buzza
Scud

Western slopes
closed during bi
season (mid Apr

Flea Rock

Long Ledge

North
Carn

Bream
Ledge

Brow of
Mincarlo

Mary Hay 1852
Figurehead in
Valhalla Museum
on Tresco

White Island
Closed during bird
breeding season
(mid April–mid Aug)

Mincarlo

PAGE 59

67

Looking across Old Grimsby Harbour from Rushy Point to St Helen's and Round Island

4. Tresco, St Helen's, Teän and Round Island

Scilly's holy isles

EOPLE TRAVEL FROM ALL OVER THE WORLD to visit **Tresco Abbey Gardens** and it's by far the most visited of Scilly's off-islands. The gardens are a northern sanctuary for subtropical and southern hemisphere plants. They thrive here because the islands are bathed in the warmth of the Gulf Stream, a current of seawater that flows northeast across the Atlantic from the Caribbean. As a consequence, winters are exceptionally mild and frosts are rare. Gales are a greater danger and Tresco is planted with sweeping shelter belts of trees to protect the sensitive plants from being scalded by salt-laden winter winds.

The Abbey Gardens are laid out around the ruins of a small abbey church that stood here between the 12th and 14th centuries. Christian foundations had been established on **St Helen's** and **Teän** (as well as on Tresco and other parts of Scilly) as early as the 6th or 7th centuries AD. This is a period the Cornish call *The Coming of the Saints,* when Celtic men and women from Ireland and Wales moved through Cornwall and Scilly establishing tiny chapels and hermitages on remote cliffs and coves. So many foundations existed here that these northern off-islands were described as a 'confederacy of hermits'.

That long tradition of seclusion and solitude was carried into the 19th and 20th centuries by the lighthouse keepers of **Round Island**. The sea immediately northwest of St Helen's and Round Island is particularly turbulent and, despite being so close to the main islands, they could find themselves marooned for days beyond the end of their watch by the stormy waters around their island. On nearby **St Helen's** in the 18th century, passengers and crew from ships suspected of being infected with disease were forcibly quarantined at the **Pest House**, made to wait on their fate on what must have seemed a terrifying but strangely beautiful desert island.

ROUND ISLAND, TEÄN, ST HELEN'S
Sightseeing trips circle this group and will occasionally land on Teän or St Helen's. Round Island is closed all year.

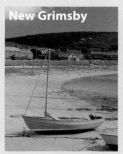

New Grimsby

TRESCO
Frequent ferries serve Tresco from St Mary's. Landing is at **New Grimsby** and **Carn Near Quay**. There are less frequent landings at **Old Grimsby**, mostly for boats from St Martin's. Any queries, go to the Estate Office at Abbey Farm. A morning landing on Tresco can be combined with an afternoon trip to Bryher or Samson (the same boat often lands on all three, one after another). Ferries are run by Tresco Boat Services.

FOOD AND DRINK
New Inn, **Ruin Beach Cafe** at Old Grimsby, **Flying Boat Restaurant** at Abbey Farm, cafe at **Abbey Gardens** and **Tresco Stores & Deli**.

BEACHES
The southern part of Tresco is really just one long beach. **Pentle Bay** is many people's favourite.

Tree ferns in the Abbey Gardens

Tresco
A little piece of Eden in the Atlantic

**Cromwell's Castle with
King Charles' Castle above**

Tresco nestles snugly in the heart of the northern off-islands and is protected on all but its northern tip by its immediate neighbours, Bryher, St Helen's and St Martin's. Landing is usually at **New Grimsby Quay**. From here you can choose to head in three different directions, north to the wild and exposed high ground of **Castle Down**, east to the velvety softness of the coast around **Old Grimsby** and **Pentle Bay** or south past **Tresco Gallery** and towards the **Abbey Gardens**. Ferries for the late afternoon return to St Mary's will often pick up from **Carn Near Quay** on the southern tip of the island.

The North End – Castle Down, Cromwell's Castle and Piper's Hole

It's just a few steps from the ferry landing at New Grimsby Quay to the coast path north to Cromwell's Castle. On one side and above you sits the granite carn of Braiden Rock and on the other side and below you lie the calm waters of New Grimsby Sound. This inlet is one of the safest anchorages in Scilly. It's protected by high ground on both sides so is not as vulnerable as other, more open anchorages to sudden shifts in wind direction. It's always busy with yachts in the summer. In the past, getting larger sailing ships in and out could be a problem if the wind was light or from the wrong direction. They would be drawn along by ropes fixed through giant iron rings on the rocks at the mouth of the Sound (said to be still in place), steadying the ship as it approached. The small set of rock-cut steps at Braiden Rock were used during World War II as a place for secret agents to embark on Breton fishing boats so that they could be infiltrated into France. The strategic value of New Grimsby Sound is illustrated by the presence of

Kettle
MV Poleire 1970
Kettle
Point
Piper's
Hole
Cork
Porth
NEW GRIMSBY SOUND

Mentos
1861
Gun Hole
Little
Kettle
Gimble
Point
Gun
Hill
Gun
Well
Cairns
Old tin
prospecting pits
Entrance
Graves
Tregarthen
Hill
Cairn
Cemetery
North End
Pollock
Rock
King Charles'
Castle
Cromwell's
Castle
Cairns
Castle Down
Castle
Porth
Beacon
Hill
Loo
Frenchman's
Point
Braiden
Steps
Braiden
Rock
Point
Carn
Ne
Grim
The
Point
New Grimsb
(high water
Plumb
Island
Plumb
Rocks
App
Po

not one, but two castles.
King Charles' Castle (and the
Blockhouse at Old Grimsby)
were built in about 1550 to
deter French and Spanish raids. In
1648, after the English Civil War had
ended, Scilly took part in a rebellion
against Parliament and the islands
became a base for Royalist privateers
attacking ships on the Western Approaches.
This upset the Dutch so much that in spring
1651 Admiral Van Tromp of the Dutch Navy
arrived to demand compensation for losses and to
put an end to the attacks. Finding no satisfaction he
declared war on Scilly and proceeded to blockade the
islands. Parliament, fearing that the islands might fall to
a foreign power, hastily sent its own force under Admiral
Blake to subdue the rebels and placate the Dutch.

Blake's force, knowing the defences on the Garrison
would be too strong to risk a head-on attack, landed instead
near Old Grimsby and after a few testy skirmishes, overcame
Royalist resistance in the Blockhouse and King Charles' Castle
to set up an artillery battery at Carn Near (Oliver's Battery).
Blockade in place, the Royalists were unable to resupply the
Star Castle and it soon capitulated. The Parliamentarian forces
set about constructing Cromwell's Castle in 1651. This was better
sited to deter enemy shipping from entering New Grimsby
Sound. Curiously, Admiral Van Tromp's declaration of war was
never officially rescinded and in 1986 the Dutch ambassador was
invited to the islands to conclude a peace between Scilly and
Holland – which he did. At 335 years, it is one of the longest, if most
uneventful wars in history.

Piper's Hole, on the far north of Tresco, is worth a visit. It's a
long, deep cave with an internal pool that goes back fifty metres into
the cliffs. Nearby, the down is covered with old tin prospecting pits.
They follow a vein of quartz and continue across to the inlet between
Gimble Point and Pollock Rock. Tregarthen Hill has fine views and a
well-preserved entrance grave on the southern side of the summit.
From here you can either follow the coast to Old Grimsby and lunch
in the Ruin Beach Cafe, or walk across the high ground to Beacon Hill
and back to New Grimsby Quay.

GRIMSBY SOUND

Sophia 1783
Coal Ledge
Coal Porth

Aurora 1784

ST HELEN'S POOL

St Helen's Porth

Kip...
Ca...

West Porth

North Isle

Old Man
South Isle

St Theona's C...
Early Christian C7...

Little Kittern

Northwethel

Cairns

The Tolmen

Entrance Graves

Raven's Rock

Crow's Island

Round Rock
Foreman's Island

Endeavour 1781

Merchant's Point

Gimble Point

Merchant's Rock

Delf 1831

Hotel Beach

Higher Ledge

Middle Ledge

Closed during bird breeding season (mid April–mid Aug)

Peashopper Island

Long Ledge

Little Cheese Rock

Middle Carn

Porth Mellin Carn

Long Point
(low water)

Trafford Rock

Lump of Clay Ledge

Chinks

Norrard

Raven Porth

Ray Island
(high water)

Tide Rock

OLD GRIMSBY HARBOUR

Cook's Bar

BACK LANE

Old Grimsby

Green Porth

Block House Point

Sch

Hall

Cook's Rock

Blockhouse Beach

The Blockhouse

Cradle Point

Rushy Point

Tea Ledge

Dolphin Town

Dolphin House

Glen Cottage

TOMMY'S HILL

Smugglers Cottage

Boro Beach

Rushy Porth

New Inn

Timothy's Corner

Cairns

Tresco

Cairns

Vane Hill

Dump

Racket Town Carn

BOROUGH ROAD

Channel Rocks

Bay Row
Abbey Farm

RACKET TOWN LN

Racket Town

Middle Down

Borough

Parting Carn

Lizard Point

Hide

Great Pool

POOL ROAD

Hide

Pentle House

Rowesfield Cottage

Pentle Bay

APPLETREE ROAD

b

Cairns

ABBEY DRIVE

Abbey Wood

Tresco Abbey

PENZANCE ROAD

Great Pentle Rock

Abbey Hill

Abbey Garden

Valhalla

Abbey Pool

Messenger 1860

Heliport

Abbey Green

Great Rock

Skirt Island

Appletree Carn

Appletree Banks

Figtree Rocks

Great Rock Beach

Bounty Ledge

Green Island

Appletree Bay

Rushy Bank

Crab's Ledge

Sea Carn

Bathinghouse Porth

Broad Ledge

Tobaccoman's Point

CARN NEAR ROAD

Chinks

CHANNEL

Oliver's Battery

Figtree Ledge

Yellow Ledge

Long Crow

Carn Near

Carn Near Quay
(low water landing)

Crow Point

Nikau palms

The East Coast – Old Grimsby, The Blockhouse, Pentle Bay

This is a straightforward walk along the eastern shore of the island from New Grimsby to Carn Near. The easiest way to get to Old Grimsby is to follow the road past the New Inn to Dolphin Town and Old Grimsby. You can lunch in the beach cafe, then simply follow the coast south to Green Porth. The Blockhouse was built to protect Old Grimsby Harbour and St Helen's Pool. From here it's one glorious beach all the way along to Pentle Bay to Carn Near Quay.

The South End – Abbey Gardens and Valhalla

The most direct route to the Abbey Gardens from New Grimsby Quay is to follow the road past Tresco Gallery to Abbey Farm. From here follow either Pool Road or Abbey Drive beside the Great Pool. Tresco Abbey has its origins in the 12th century when all the religious foundations on the northern part of Scilly were granted to the Benedictine monks of Tavistock Abbey. There was probably already a religious foundation here when they arrived – similar to the sites on Teän and St Helen's. An inscribed gravestone that fits the period sits near one of the arches of the Abbey, and when the gardens were laid out in the 1830s, graves were found nearby. The name of that original saint has been lost and it was the monks of Tavistock Abbey who dedicated this site to St Nicholas, the patron saint of seafarers. Although little remains of the priory church it must have been a substantial building by Scillonian standards, even though it was probably home to only a handful of monks at any one time.

Scilly was extremely vulnerable to raids by pirates and Vikings. The priory and chapels were especially tempting targets and suffered repeated raids. The monks didn't take it all lying

Figurehead in Valhalla from the *Palinurus* wrecked on the Lion Rock off the northern tip of St Martin's in December 1848. She was from Demerara with a cargo of rum, part of which was saved by locals. All her crew were lost.

Abbey Gardens

down though; they had their own zero tolerance policy. In 1209 they are said to have beheaded 120 pirates in a single afternoon. This was probably a rare victory and the monks finally abandoned Tresco in the 14th century.

When Augustus Smith took over the lease of the islands from the Duchy of Cornwall in 1834 he built what has become a world famous subtropical garden in the ruins of the old abbey. Many of the original plants were purchased from passing sailing ships returning to Britain from the southern hemisphere. The whole garden is protected by long shelter belts of trees and hedges. Behind them you'll find the beautiful blue agapanthus and protea both natives of South Africa, echiums more commonly found in the Canary Isles, Nikau palms and tree ferns from New Zealand and Chilean wine palms. The whole place is a gardener's paradise. Dotted around the gardens are interesting objects gathered from the surrounding islands. The most ancient is said to be a Bronze Age holed stone or menhir. There is also a Romano-British inscribed stone and a Roman altar found in a well beneath the Garrison wall on St Mary's (page 16). The altar side panels are carved with low reliefs. One is a dagger and one an axe, so this was possibly used for making sacrifices. Within the garden walls at Valhalla, there is an impressive collection of figureheads salvaged from ships lost on the islands along with cannons salvaged from the seabed. At least one cannon belongs to *HMS Association* lost on the Western Rocks in 1707. Nearby stands the coal brazier that was used to illuminate the old lighthouse on St Agnes (page 42).

Recommended walks Tresco

Most boats land at **New Grimsby**. From here you can head north on to Castle Downs, head over to Old Grimsby and the east coast or wander south to the Abbey Gardens. Ferries back to St Mary's usually pick up in the late afternoon from **Carn Near Quay** on the southern tip of the island.

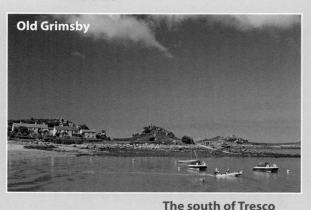
Old Grimsby

The North End

This is the wild and windy part of Tresco. Exposed and uncultivated but with lots to explore – two castles, cairns and tombs plus a deep natural cave. Makes a good morning walk followed by lunch and a visit to the Abbey Gardens.

At **New Grimsby Quay** take the coast path north between the buildings at the end of the quay to **Braiden Carn** and **Cromwell's Castle**. From here, you have the choice of following the coast to **Kettle Point** or walking up to **King Charles' Castle** and on to Castle Down. The deep natural cave at **Piper's Hole** is one of the more accessible caves on Scilly. **Tregarthen's Hill** has a fine entrance grave on its summit and good views. From here you can shortcut back to New Grimsby by following the high ground to **Beacon Hill** and **Dial Rocks** or, follow the coast at low level to **Gimble Porth.** **Merchant Rock** has good views over Northwethel. Grab some lunch at the Ruin Beach Cafe or walk back to New Grimsby along **Back Lane** or via **Dolphin Town** to the New Inn for a pint while you wait for the ferry to arrive.

....

Distance
4.7km (3 miles) from New Grimsby Quay to Kettle Point, Old Grimsby and back again. Add about 3km (1¾ miles) to walk down to Carn Near Quay.

Places to picnic and swim
Castle Down Brow to picnic, Green Porth to swim.

The south of Tresco

Most people simply follow the coast road to the Abbey Gardens but consider walking over to Old Grimsby and then along Borough Road and Abbey Pool. Combined with a visit to the Abbey Gardens this fills a whole day.

From **New Grimsby Quay** take **Back Lane** to **Norrard** and **Old Grimsby**. From here you can wander up to **Merchant Rock** with its views. Lunch at the cafe on the beach. Then walk along **Green Porth** to the **Blockhouse**. Most people follow the coast path along the dunes to **Pentle Bay**, but **Borough Road** is a nice inland walk too. At this point you have the option to turn inland at **Abbey Pool** to the **Abbey Gardens**. Otherwise, continue to **Carn Near Quay** for your ferry or back along Abbey Drive to **New Grimsby Quay**.

....

Distance
*4.5km (2¾ miles) from **New Grimsby Quay** to **Old Grimsby** and along the coast to **Carn Near Quay**.*
*3km (1¾ miles) direct from **Old Grimsby Quay** to the **Abbey Gardens** and then on to **Carn Near Quay**.*

Places to picnic and swim
Lots of choice but Pentle Bay

Around Borough Farm

St Helen's, Teän and Round Island
A confederacy of hermits

St Helen's and Round Island

Sightseeing trips circle these islands to watch puffins and other seabirds but also to view close up the dramatic cliffs of **Round Island** and **Men-a-vaur**. Inter-island ferries don't make regular landings but private charter boats and kayaks frequently land on **Teän** and **St Helen's**. Judging by the remains, this landscape was widely settled in prehistory. Stone field walls, now mostly tumbled down, cover parts of **St Helen's**, **Northwethel** and **Teän**. They hint at how the prehistoric landscape might have looked 2,000 to 3,000 years ago: small dispersed farms made up of a few simple round huts with a handful of fields, bracken-covered hillsides leading up to granite ridges and carns where the tombs of the ancestors are placed.

Although this is one of the more remote parts of Scilly, **Teän** and **St Helen's** can claim a surprisingly long history of occupation compared to other places on the islands, many parts of which were abandoned for long periods in the past. Certainly, most people who have lived in this part of Scilly have had to become inured to a solitary and withdrawn existence, either out of choice or of necessity. The most venerated residents are a pair of 7th or 8th century Celtic Christian saints, **Theona** and **Elidius**, who sought out isolated places like this to found their religious communities. For the lighthouse keepers of **Round Island**, solitude came with their job and the rocky inaccessibility of their island. For the in-patients of the 18th century quarantine station on **St Helen's** – known as the **Pest House** – they were compelled by law to put ashore here to see out the course of their contagion. All these islands retain an atmosphere of seclusion.

77

St Helen's and the Pest House

The name St Helen's is a corruption of St Elidius, a male Celtic saint and hermit who lived and died here in the 7th or 8th century AD. The remains of his original, circular hermit cell are still clearly visible along with the rough circular wall that enclosed the holy precinct. In most Cornish churches these sorts of original structures were lost as the site continued to develop, although the line of the circular or oval boundary is often retained – an echo of the original foundation. Here the site is left in its original form and with its original buildings – an intriguing snapshot of what many mainland church sites must have looked like more than a thousand years ago.

Apart from his name, all we know about Elidius was that he was said to be the son of a British king and a bishop in the Celtic church. He was certainly well thought of because the site, just like Teän, continued in occupation for many centuries after his death, and in the 11th century, 300 years after his death, a small stone chapel and a number of smaller rectangular buildings were built for a religious community, probably by the monks of Tavistock Abbey soon after they settled on Tresco. Inside the tiny stone chapel is an altar with a hidden recess for the holy relics of Elidius and a grave near the church is thought to belong to the man himself. The site seems to have fallen into disuse and ruin in the 14th or 15th century but a service is still held here on 8th August each year (or the nearest Sunday) to celebrate his feast day. A display board at the site gives a history of the ruins and has pictures of some of the artefacts found during the excavations which are on show at the Island Museum in Hugh Town on St Mary's.

A few hundred metres west of St Elidius' Sanctuary, and clearly visible from passing boats, are the roofless walls of an 18th century isolation hospital known locally as the **Pest House**. Passengers and crew from ships suspected of carrying disease were landed here. Many had already survived weeks at sea in ships infected with cholera, typhus or the plague – often contracted in the souqs of North Africa and the Mediterranean. Sometimes the ship itself was quarantined in St Helen's Pool. Victims stayed here until they either died or recovered. Those that died were buried nearby and include a naval surgeon, James Gorse, who died of cholera when serving here. Prehistoric fields lie west of the hospital and they were re-used by the in-patients.

Cormorant

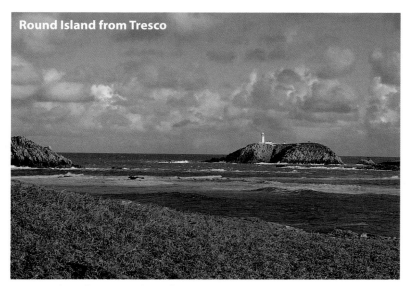
Round Island from Tresco

Teän and St Theona's Chapel

This small island (pronounced *tee-an)* is a favourite spot for picnics having that very attractive Scillonian mix of sandy beach, rocky cove and craggy hill all within touching distance of each other. The seaweed-covered foundations of prehistoric hut circles and field walls stand out against the sandy bottom of East and West Porth, and the crumbling remains of St Theona's Chapel and Teän Farm sit next to each other at the top of the beach at East Porth.

When St Theona's Chapel was excavated in the 1950s, sixteen early Christian graves were found. The original 7th or 8th century chapel was probably constructed in wood and has left little trace. It was replaced by a stone building in the 12th century; the new altar and east wall were located directly over a group of three of the early graves. One of the skeletons uncovered here was an elderly, toothless woman, possibly St Theona herself. It looks as if the new chapel was sited so that St Theona's head would be right under the altar. Other later graves included four children, some suffering from leprosy.

In the 17th and 18th centuries the Nance family from Falmouth introduced kelp burning to Scilly. The seaweed was cut, dried on the shore then burnt in shallow stone-lined pits to produce soda and potash for use in the glass and soap industries, giving old glass its characteristic greenish tinge. It took about twenty tons of seaweed to produce just one ton of kelp. The most obvious building is the 18th century Teän Farm. The island was still grazed by cattle in the 1950s. The animals swam from St Martin's roped to the side of a punt.

Men-a-vaur and Golden Ball Brow

Like Hanjague and Castle Bryher, Men-a-vaur is a very meaty pile of rock. It looks impressive enough from a distance, but close up, its frighteningly shear sides look extremely scary. The rock is cut by deep ravines just wide enough for a small dinghy to pass through on a calm sea. Puffins and other seabirds breed here turning the rock into a seabird skyscraper in the summer. Golden Ball Brow, like Round Island and Men-a-vaur, sits on the edge of an underwater cliff and is prone to huge seas and freak waves that for a time attracted extreme surfers.

Northwethel

Like its neighbours this island has traces of prehistoric field walls and round huts. They are usually hidden under a carpet of bracken. The southeastern ridge has a collection of cairns and at least one entrance grave. The prominent carn called the Tolmen acts as a mark for local fishermen.

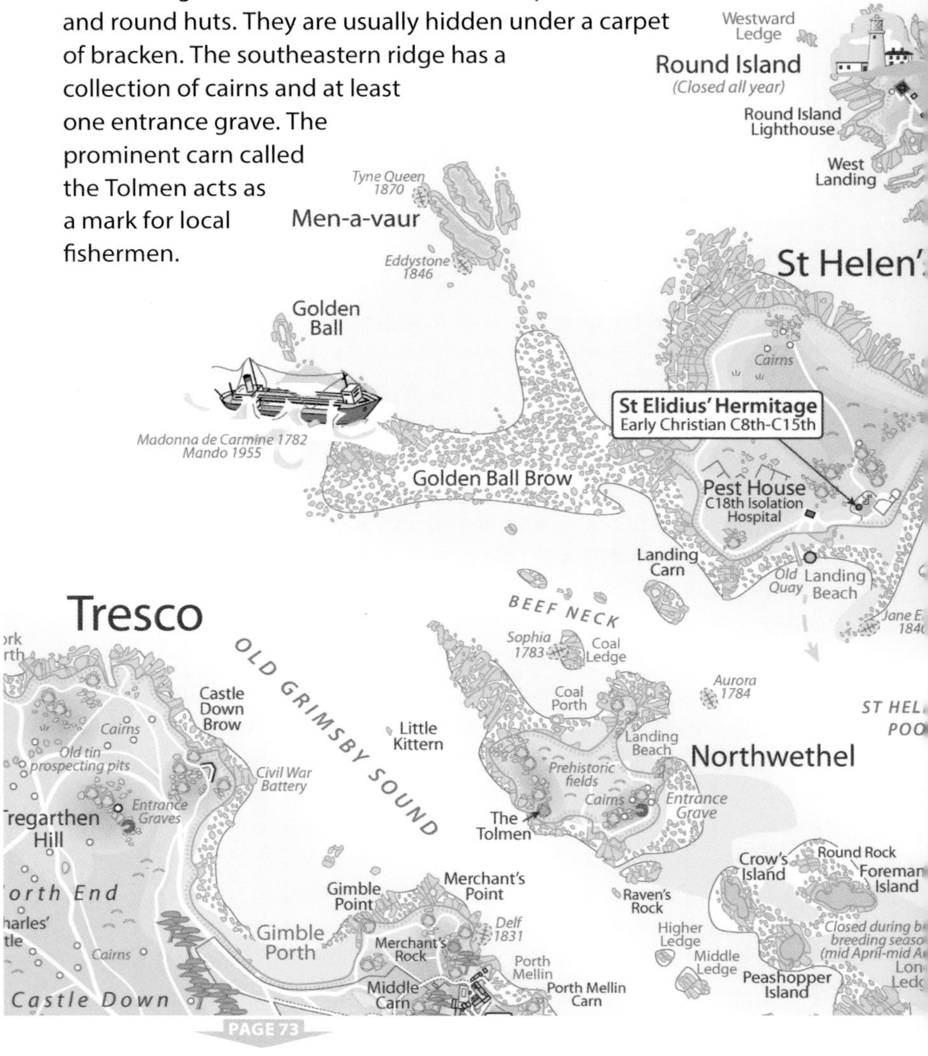

Westward Ledge

Round Island
(Closed all year)

Round Island Lighthouse

West Landing

Tyne Queen 1870

Men-a-vaur

Eddystone 1846

St Helen'

Golden Ball

Cairns

St Elidius' Hermitage
Early Christian C8th-C15th

Madonna de Carmine 1782
Mando 1955

Golden Ball Brow

Pest House
C18th Isolation Hospital

Landing Carn

Old Landing Quay Beach

Jane E 1840

Tresco

BEEF NECK

Sophia 1783
Coal Ledge

Coal Porth

Aurora 1784

ST HEL POO

Castle Down Brow

OLD GRIMSBY SOUND

Little Kittern

Landing Beach

Northwethel

Cairns

Old tin prospecting pits

Civil War Battery

Prehistoric fields

Cairns

Entrance Grave

Tregarthen Hill

Entrance Graves

The Tolmen

Crow's Island

Round Rock

Foreman Island

orth End

harles' tle

Cairns

Gimble Point

Merchant's Point

Raven's Rock

Higher Ledge

Closed during b breeding seaso (mid April-mid A Lon

Gimble Porth

Delf 1831

Merchant's Rock

Porth Mellin

Middle Ledge

Peashopper Island

Middle Carn

Porth Mellin Carn

Castle Down

PAGE 73

Round Island Lighthouse

The lighthouse became operational in 1887 completing a ring of warning lights around Scilly. Its lantern stands almost sixty metres above sea level and is clearly visible from Land's End forty-five kilometres away (1 white flash every 10 seconds). The island sits right on the edge of deep water making the island vulnerable to very big waves, and it can be completely lost in clouds of sea spray in rough weather. Following a storm in 1886, workers found limpets had been thrown onto the roofs of buildings fifty metres above sea level. This explains why, for such a tall island, it has so little in the way of greenery. Lighthouse keepers who lived here (it's now automated) had to bring baskets of soil with them to be able to grow fresh vegetables. Since the island was cleared of rats by the Isles of Scilly Wildlife Trust its population of seabirds, including Manx shearwaters and storm petrels, has increased greatly. Round Island is closed to visitors all year.

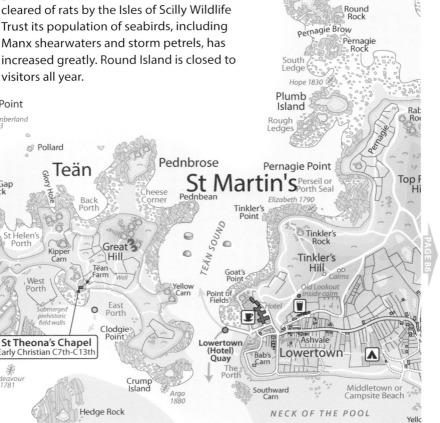

Lion Rock

Palinurus 1848 Figurehead in Valhalla Museum on Tresco

West Withian

Withian Carns

Pernagie Isle

Round Rock

Pernagie Brow

Pernagie Rock

South Ledge

Hope 1830

Plumb Island

Rab Ro

Rough Ledges

Pernagie

Didley's Point

Duke of Cumberland 1773

Pollard

ST HELEN'S GAP

Teän

Glory Hole

East Gap Rock

Pednbrose

Pednbean

Pernagie Point

St Martin's

Perseil or Porth Seal

Top P Hi

Elizabeth 1790

Cheese Corner

Back Porth

Tinkler's Point

St Helen's Porth

Kipper Carn

Great Hill

Teän Farm

Well

TEÄN SOUND

Tinkler's Rock

Tinkler's Hill

Cairns

North Isle

West Porth

Yellow Carn

Goat's Point

Old Lookout inside cairn

Man outh Isle

Submerged prehistoric field walls

East Porth

Point of Fields

Hotel

St Theona's Chapel
Early Christian C7th–C13th

Clodgie Point

Lowertown (Hotel) Quay

Bab's Carn

Ashvale

Lowertown

Endeavour 1781

Crump Island

Argo 1880

The Porth

Southward Carn

Middletown or Campsite Beach

Hedge Rock

NECK OF THE POOL

Yello

PAGE 86

The sparkling water of Scilly's inner sea – looking over to Teän from The Porth at Lowertown

5. St Martin's and the Eastern Isles

Sunny hillsides and splendid carns

THIS CORNER OF SCILLY BENEFITS GREATLY from being sheltered by St Mary's and Tresco and, as a result, **St Martin's** is just a little greener than the other islands. Its south-facing hillsides are natural sun-traps so the hedges and gardens are full of subtropical plants, and even in early spring or late autumn, the ground is full of warmth. The northern coast is a much more rugged and wild place. It looks over the sea to Land's End, and from **Chapel Down** in the evening, the scene is lit up by the twinkle and flash of at least five lighthouses that mark the many dangers between Scilly and the mainland. This has been a busy shipping lane for two thousand years.

The **Eastern Isles** lie just a few hundred metres southeast of St Martin's. Sightseeing boats come to watch the seals that haul-out on the rocks around **Menawethan** and **Innisvouls**. All these isles are uninhabited now but the remains of prehistoric fields and round huts show up on **Nornour** and its neighbour, **Great Ganilly**. Most spectacularly, a Roman shrine for mariners was uncovered on the beach at **Nornour** after a storm in 1962. **Arthur** belongs to a select group of places on Scilly that prehistoric man chose as ritual sites – each one of its three hills is topped by tombs.

On a normal low tide, ferries have to weave back and forth around the sand banks and bars of **Martin's Flats** to get through to **Highertown Quay**, and on the lowest tides of the year the sand banks are completely impassable by boat. When it floods back in, the sea creates a shallow lagoon stretching between St Martin's, Guther's Island and Tresco. This is one of the loveliest sights in Scilly. The white sand beneath the surface of the sea gives it an extraordinary sparkle perhaps best experienced by hiring a sea kayak to explore the many rocks, ledges and islands.

EASTERN ISLES
Sightseeing boats don't land on the Eastern Isles but do come in close to see the seals. Private charter boats and yachts land at Nornour and Arthur Quay.

Lowertown Quay

ST MARTIN'S
Ferries from St Mary's and other islands land at **Highertown Quay** and **Lowertown (Hotel) Quay**.

FOOD AND DRINK
Karma St Martin's hotel and Seven Stones Inn at Lowertown. Post Office Stores, Island Bakery and Polreath Cafe in Highertown. Adam's Fish & Chips (evenings) at East'ard and Little Arthur Cafe & Bistro.

BEACHES
The whole southern coast of St Martin's is one long beach. The best family beaches are **Campsite Beach**, **The Porth** and **Par Beach**. On the northern coast **Great Bay** and **Little Bay** are very popular and have more rugged scenery. **Perpitch** and **Old Quay** are quieter spots.

The rugged northern cliffs of St Martin's looking over Bull's Porth to Burnt Hill and St Martin's Head – Land's End is just visible on the horizon

St Martin's and White Island
Scilly's verdant isle

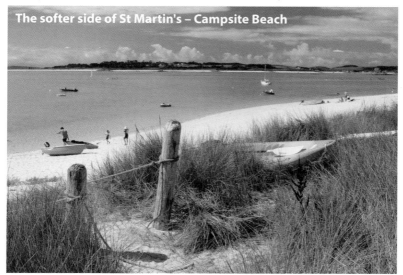

The softer side of St Martin's – Campsite Beach

No other island on Scilly offers such contrasting faces to the world as St Martin's. From the air, the island forms a great crescent shape on the northeastern edge of Scilly and is split in two on its long axis by a ridge of high ground that runs the whole length of the island from **Top Rock** to **Chapel Down**. South of this watershed about 140 people live in the farms and settlements of **Lowertown**, **Middletown** and **Highertown**, linked together by St Martin's only road. These sunny south-facing slopes are covered in a patchwork of hedges and narrow fields that nestle in the natural hollows of the hillsides. Fields of agapanthus, lilies, daffodils and cabbages run down to merge with the sand dunes. The north coast is very different: wild and weatherbeaten, an uncultivated landscape punctuated by splendid granite carns and dramatic headlands – **Top Rock**, **Turfy Hill**, **Burnt Hill** and **St Martin's Head** – the grandest coastal scenery on Scilly.

The sheltered coast – Highertown Quay, Cruther's Hill and Old Quay
As the ferry comes in to Highertown Quay it passes beneath Cruther's Hill and although it's a distinctive-looking hill, you get no inkling of just how good the views are from its summit. The views only really reveal themselves when you're standing on the top, so many visitors miss this treat altogether as they wander past on their way to Highertown. But if you stop at the sharp corner at the top of Par Hill and turn left down the rough track you'll soon come across the path to the summit. Cruther's Hill is one of those distinctive rocky places so valued by prehistoric Scillonians and each of its three mini-summits has its own tombs. The entrance grave on the middle summit is the clearest as

Palinurus 1848
Figurehead in Valhalla
Museum on Tresco

• Brewer

Lion Rock

• Baker

West
Withian

Shag
Point

Tabasco
1879

Closed during bird
breeding season
(April–Sept inclusive)

Withian
Carns

White
Island

Entrance
grave

Stony
Porth

Underland Girt

SS Aksai
1875

East Withian

Pernagie
Isle

Cairns

Porth
Morran
Quay

Chad Point

Chad Girt

Round
Rock

Permorran
or
Porth Morran

Camper Porth

Black Rock
Ledges

Pernagie Brow

Kelp pits

Pernagie
Rock

Camper
Point

Camper
Carn

South
Ledge

Hope 1830

Butter
Porth

Rushy
Carn

Jacky's Point

Plumb
Island

Pernagie

White Island Bar

Anthony

Rabbit
Rocks

Rough
Ledges

Mazes

Aunt Elsie's Rock

Little
Ledge

Lofarno
1902

Pednbrose

Round
Bowl Rock

The
Cove

Merrick
Rock

Pernagie Point

Entrance
grave

Scilly Point

Great Merrick
Ledge

Perseil or
Porth Seal

Top Rock
Hill

Top
Rock

Little Bay

Little Le
Mack
Rock

Pednbean

Elizabeth 1790

Little Merrick
Ledge

Tinkler's
Point

Cairn

ese
her

Yellow
Carn

Thongyore
Ledge

Tinkler's
Rock

Sheep
Ledge

ST MARTIN'
BAY

Goat's
Point

Tinkler's
Hill

Cairns

The
Plains

Great Bay

Point of
Fields

Old lookout
inside cairn

Hotel

Hotel

Lowertown
(Hotel)
Quay

Ashvale

Middletown

Frenchman's
Graves

Bab's
Carn

Lowertown

Plains
House

Prescella
Well

Crump
Island

Argo 1880

The
Porth

Hall

Southward
Carn

Middletown or
Campsite Beach

Yellow
Rock
Carn

Knackyboy
Carn
Entrance
grave

SCHOOL

Fire
Stn

Ch

NECK OF THE POOL

Yellow
Rock

Lawrance's Fields

LANE

onlon

John Martin's
Ledge

Dog
Ledge

Round
Rock

Jack's
Ledge

Forester
1883

Lawrance's
Brow

Carrion
Rocks

Carron
Farm

Cair
Cruthers

West Broad
Ledge

Stephen's
Ledge

LAWRANCE'S
BAY

Old Quay
Beach

Broad
Ledge

MARTIN'S FLATS

Moths
Ledge

Pigs
Ledge

Old
Quay

Entrance
graves

Furnace
1758

St Martin's

Branders
Rock

Crows Nest

Wra
Ledge

Lawrance'
Ledge

TEÄN SOUND

SOUND

its roof slabs have been removed and the passage cleared out. This is one of the best places to appreciate how different the landscape of Scilly was in prehistory. When these tombs were built 3,500 years ago, the sea lapped on the far shores of the Eastern Isles and instead of the shallow inland sea of today, the view in front of you to Tresco and St Mary's was a mix of farmland, dunes and salt marsh, perhaps with the carns of Guther's Island rising above the tops of the trees.

Return to the track and head down to Old Quay. This was the harbour for St Martin's before Highertown Quay was built and is one of Scilly's secret and special places. Recent excavations, as part of the Neolithic Stepping Stones project, have uncovered thousands of flint and pottery fragments and the post holes of a building from the Neolithic Age (about 5,500 years ago). This must have been one of the very first settlements on Scilly, probably a seasonal camp for hunters rather than a farm. There's no path along the coast from here, so if the tide's out, you'll have to walk along the shore towards Lawrance's Fields where you can join the coast path. If the tide's in, return up the track to Highertown.

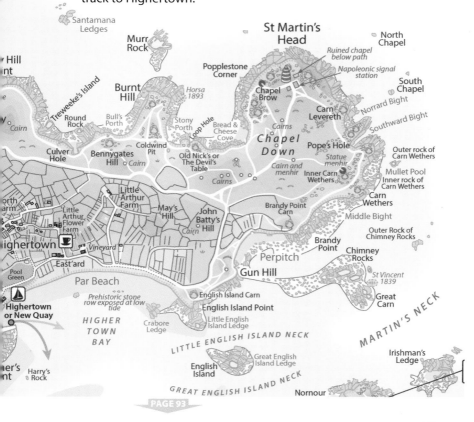

PAGE 93

87

Island Bakery at Highertown

Highertown

This is the main settlement on St Martin's. A gallery and bakery stand on Moo Green with Polreath Cafe and the Island Stores on the main road. Behind the cafe, around Signal Rock, is a perfect example of what in Cornwall you would call a 'town place' – a shared urban space between three or four farms in a small settlement. Despite its small size, it's a direct relation of the village greens and urban squares on the mainland. A place where the old men would sit and pass the time.

Lowertown, Tinkler's Hill, White Island and St Martin's Bay

After lunch in the pub or hotel at Lowertown, head up to Tinkler's Hill and on to the north coast of the island. It's worth diverting from the main path to take in the views from Tinkler's Rock over to Teän and Round Island. Then follow the path to Pernagie and Butter Porth. Except for a few tumbled field walls, this landscape has very few signs of human occupation. It's rare to find this in Cornwall or Scilly, which have very dispersed patterns of settlement so that there are very few places where you can stand and see no house at all. I think this is why this part of St Martin's is reminiscent of a Scottish Island.

White Island is connected to St Martin's by a boulder bar for an hour-or-so either side of low water. It's actually easier to visit by boat or kayak than to scramble over the slippery rocks. Once you're on the island, a fine entrance grave sits on the high ground to the north and there's a good example of a kelp pit sitting just above the beach at Permorran. These were used throughout the islands in the 18th century to burn seaweed to made soda ash for the glass industry.

Top Rock has good views over St Martin's Bay to Chapel Down, and the nearby beaches at Little Bay and Great Bay are popular places for family picnics and swimming. Frenchman's Graves is said to be the burial ground for the crew of an unnamed ship wrecked on the rocks below. Cliff burial for bodies washed ashore after a wreck was common practice in the 17th and 18th centuries and was especially true for those who had the temerity to be at the same time Catholic, Republican and French – an unpalatable combination at the time.

Looking over Great Bay to Top Rock and White Island

The exposed coast – Chapel Down, St Martin's Head, Seven Stones
There may have been some sort of beacon here as far back as
Roman times, possibly associated with the shrine on Nornour.
The foundations of a small Medieval chapel are visible below the
daymark. Religious houses set up and maintained lights on prominent
headlands throughout Britain and because of this, many are named
after a saint. The beacon was usually manned by a solitary monk
living in the chapel itself. The chapel was robbed of stone during
the construction of the daymark in 1683 and again when the nearby
Napoleonic signal station was built. This was used to relay semaphore
messages to Royal Navy ships standing offshore ready to pounce
on any passing 'Frenchie'. The station was replaced after only a few
years by the purpose-built, circular semaphore tower at Telegraph on
St Mary's.

Look northeast from here and you'll see waves breaking on the
Hard Lewis Rocks and, if it's really rough, over the Seven Stones Reef
ten kilometres away. The reef is said to have been the site of the City
of Lions, capital of the Lost Land of Lyonesse (see page 10). In 1967
this was the site of the wreck of the oil tanker *Torrey Canyon* which
covered West Cornwall beaches in oil. Looking from northeast to
south on a clear evening you can see the Sevenstones Lightvessel (3
flashes every 30 seconds), Pendeen Light (4 flashes every 15 seconds),
Longships Lighthouse (5 second flash followed by 5 seconds dark) and
close to each other – Lizard Lighthouse (1 flash every 3 seconds) and
the Wolf Rock Lighthouse (1 white flash every 15 seconds).

Recommended walks St Martin's

Ferries land at both **Highertown** and **Lowertown Quays**. Ideally you'll be able to land at one, stroll along the coast or island road and be picked up at the other. Food shop, cafe and bakery in Highertown. Hotel and pub at Lowertown.

The shipping daymark on St Martin's Head

Chapel Down and the wild east of St Martin's

This is a great walk on a blowy day with views over to the Seven Stones and Land's End. It's a particularly good evening walk to see all the lighthouses flashing (see map page 10).

From **Highertown Quay** head across **Pool Green** following the track above **Par Beach** and past the vineyard. At **Gun Hill** you can turn off the main path to follow the coast path at low level to **Perpitch**. Otherwise continue on the main track to **Chapel Down** and **St Martin's Head**. You can drop down to **Bread and Cheese Cove** for a little shelter and a place to picnic if it's very windy. Continue to **St Martin's Head** and the daymark. From here, take the coast path to **Carn Levereth**. Just beyond **Pope's Hole** you can make a diversion inland up to the statue menhir (much eroded) but remember to return the way you came from the coast path – there's no easy path across the top of the downs. The coast path follows the cliffs at low level back to **Brandy Point**, **Perpitch** and **Gun Hill** where you rejoin the main path to **Pool Green**. Then it's time for a quick swim or a chance to sit on **Par Beach** and wait for the ferry.

Distance
4.3km (2¾ miles) from Highertown Quay.
Best picnic spots
Great Par, Bread and Cheese Cove.

Lowertown, Top Rock, the west of St Martin's

A walk along the dunes and beaches to Lowertown with a return along the rugged north coast by Tinkler's Hill and Top Rock Hill.

From **Highertown Quay** follow the road up **Par Hill** to the sharp corner at the top. From here you can turn down the track to the south and to **Cruther's Hill** and **Old Quay**. There's no coast path at Old Quay but if the tide's out you can walk along the beach to **Lawrance's Fields** and pick the path up again. Alternatively, stay with the road into **Highertown** for shop, bakery and cafes, then follow the road to **Middletown** and **Lowertown** and the chance to have some lunch. Continue to **Tinkler's Hill** and **Top Rock Hill**. Little Bay is a popular place to swim. Return to Highertown and the quay by **Plains House** or **Pound Lane**.

Distance
From Highertown Quay, it's about 2.3km (1½ miles) to Lowertown and about 6km (3¾ miles) in total if you walk around the north end of St Martin's to White Island and return to Highertown by The Plains.
Best picnic spots
Old Quay, Pernagie.

Looking north from Cruther's Hill

The Eastern Isles
Home to seals and a cult of Venus

Popular sightseeing ferries weave between these engaging small isles on their way to watch the seals that haul-out on **Menawethan** and **Innisvouls**. Sightseeing trips don't land in the Eastern Isles, although kayaks and private charter boats do come ashore on the beach south of **Nornour** and at **Arthur Quay**, mostly to look at the prehistoric tombs and huts. From mid-summer onwards most of the archaeology is submerged under bracken, so anyone wishing to visit should aim to get here in the early part of the year.

Nornour

In the early 1960s storms washed away part of the beach between Nornour and Great Ganilly exposing walling on the foreshore. Excavations then uncovered a small settlement of eight or nine round huts, the oldest dating from the Bronze Age 3,500 years ago, the youngest from about the 5th century AD. At first, there seemed nothing particularly unusual about these tumbled walls; this was an interesting prehistoric settlement, but only one of a number of similar sites on Scilly. But then, unusual objects started to turn up – Roman imperial coins, hundreds of enamelled brooches, rings and trinkets – all oddly out-of-place in the humble surroundings of a prehistoric farmstead. Most were wedged between the walling stones of a single building; others were found beneath the sand on the beach, presumably washed out by the waves.

Most revealing of all, several clay figurines of Venus were recovered. These sort of figurines were mass-produced in Roman Gaul as charms and votive offerings. The conclusion was that this site was a Roman shrine and that Nornour was a stopping-off point for ships travelling between Gaul and the Irish Sea. Nornour faces directly over to Land's End and it may have been near to the main landing place in prehistoric Scilly. It's possible that the shrine is connected with some sort of early beacon and passing ships may have called here to invoke the protection of the goddess. Like St Warna's Well on St Agnes (page 40), this might be a shrine dedicated to a native Celtic goddess. Charles Thomas suggests *Silla* or *Silus*, the water goddess who was worshipped at the thermal springs in Bath. Roman writers do talk of islands off the coast of Britain known as *Sillina* and it's probable that their geography was based on the close questioning of Roman sailors who knew these waters well. This would certainly give a neat explanation for the origin for the name Scilly. Here, however, unlike on St Agnes, the existence of the shrine was forgotten and no folk memory came down to historic times. Finds from Nornour are exhibited in the museum in Hugh Town.

PAGE 86

Old Quay Beach
Moths Ledge
Pigs Ledge
Old Quay
Cruther's Hill
Entrance Graves
Highertown or New Quay
Prehistoric stone row exposed at low tide
Crabore Ledge
HIGHER TOWN BAY
Crows Nest
Cruther's Point
Harry's Rock
Wra Ledge
Lawrance's Ledge
Excelsior 1881

St Martin's

GUTHER'S BAR
Deason's Cap
Three Rocks
Great Damasinnas
Borthse
Middle Damasinnas
Outer Damasinnas
Guther's Island
Peaked Ledge

Long Scud
Eastward Guthern
Manuel Scud
Great Ledge
Great Ganinick
Western Guthern
Ganinick Brow
Little Ganinick

Hanjague

A nineteen-metre-high pile of granite that presents an unmistakable profile on the eastern approach to the islands. Its name is pronounced *'an-jig* and translates from Cornish as the *windy rock*.

Captain Deason and the *SS Earl of Arran*

The *Earl of Arran* was one of two Penzance steamers serving Scilly that were lost in 1872. The *SS Little Western* was lost on Southward Well near Samson in October; the *Earl of Arran* on Nornour in July. Her master, Captain Deason was persuaded by one of his passengers to take a shortcut through Great English Island Neck and avoid the more usual, but longer route south of St Mary's. They had just passed inside Hanjague when a tremor rippled through the ship – she had torn a hole in her side on Irishman's Ledge. Captain Deason was forced to run the ship aground on Nornour Brow to save the ninety-two passengers on board. Her boilers sit there today. The captain is immortalised in the name of the prominent carn on Guther's Island, Deason's Cap, a mark used today by yachts and fishing boats.

The Arthurs

All three of the Arthurs have entrance graves on their summits – Middle Arthur is a particularly fine example. When these Bronze Age tombs were built this was probably a prominent headland at the entrance to one of the main landing places on ancient Scilly (see map inside the front cover).

The map shows the following labelled features:

Hanjague *(Closed all year)*

h Island Carn
ish Island Point
e English
nd Ledge
GLISH ISLAND NECK

Great
Carn

Nornour Settlement & Shrine
Iron Age/Romano-British C2th BC–C1st AD

Irishman's
Ledge

Great English
Island Ledge

GREAT ENGLISH ISLAND NECK

Nornour
Brow

Nornour

SS Gomes V
1888

Earl of Arran 1872
(boiler shows at
low water)

Round
Rock

Northward
Head

Shag
Rocks

Cairns

Inner
Shag
Rocks

Jolly
Point

ILLY
R

Mouls

Holmbush
Carn

East Porth

Great Ganilly

Black
Lump

Little Innisvouls
(Closed all year)

Little
Ganilly

West Porth

Seal
Rock

Innisvouls
Brow

INNISVOULS NECK

er
d

Southern end of
Great Ganilly closed during
bird breeding season
(mid April to mid Aug)

Goat's Hole

Great Innisvouls
(Closed all year)

Ladies'
Ledge

Ragged Island
*(Closed mid April
to mid Aug)*

Outer
Carn

LITTLE GANILLY NECK

LADIES' LEDGE NECK

MENAWETHAN NECK

Arthur Quay

Little
Arthur

Eastern
Isles

Middle
Arthur

Renny
Brow

Cairn

China
Point

Sheep
Carn

Arthur
Porth

Great
Arthur

Renny

The Hole

China
Rock

Arthur
Brow

The Peak

Entrance
Graves &
Cairns

Frenchman's Rock

Menawethan
(Closed all year)

Gauloise
1888

Arthur Head

Little Biggal

Biggal

Grey seal

The seals of the Eastern Isles

The Eastern Isles, Western and Norrard Rocks are all popular places
to watch Atlantic grey seals. They usually pup between August and
October but will haul-out and bask on the same sites throughout the
year, casting a quizzical eye over the boatloads of visitors. The cows
give an exceptionally rich milk and their pups gain up to nine kilos in
the first week after birth. After about three weeks, the pup will have
tripled in weight and is then abruptly deserted by its mother who goes
looking for a mate. Over the next two weeks the pup lives off its fat
while its sea coat grows. The bulls are more conspicuous than the cows
because of their darker coats and larger size.

Helpful information
Getting to and around Scilly

The *Scillonian* steams into Crow Sound

Information

The Tourist Information Centre is located above Porthcressa Beach in Hugh Town, St Mary's.
E: info@visitislesofscilly.com
T: (01720) 620600
www.visitislesofscilly.com

GETTING TO PENZANCE

Driving to Penzance

Head for Exeter then follow the A30 to Penzance. The A30 can be very busy on summer Saturdays and bank holiday weekends. To avoid the queues, aim to arrive on the Cornish border (about 1¼ hours from Penzance) before mid-morning or leave it until late afternoon/early evening. Driving to Exeter and flying from there avoids Cornwall's congested trains and roads in the summer.

Parking in Penzance

You can't take your car to Scilly but there is secure parking at Land's End Airport, Penzance Heliport and in various locations around Penzance. Some secure parking sites are on the outskirts of Penzance so book parking when you buy your travel tickets and make sure you arrange a shuttle bus or taxi to take you to your departure point.

Train to Penzance

Penzance Station is served by direct trains from London Paddington and the North. The Night Riviera sleeper train leaves Paddington late evening and will get you to Penzance by about 8am the following morning. A shuttle bus runs between the station and Land's End Airport (12km/7½ miles) and Penzance Heliport. You will need to book a seat in advance and should aim to leave Penzance Station one hour before your scheduled take-off time. You can also get a taxi from the station forecourt. Passengers for the *Scillonian* can simply walk along the harbour to the Lighthouse Quay.

GETTING TO SCILLY

By helicopter

A helicopter service operates from Penzance Heliport (near Sainsbury's as you come into Penzance on the A30) to St Mary's Airport and Tresco. The flight time from Penzance Heliport is about 15 minutes. On-site secure parking is available, as well as a shuttle from the train station. Bookings can be made on their website.
www.penzancehelicopters.co.uk
T: (01736) 780828

By ship and plane

The *Scillonian* usually departs Penzance at 9.15am; the return sailing leaves St Mary's at 4.30pm. The journey takes about 2¾ hours. Departure times vary depending on time of year, tide and weather. In the busiest periods, there is also a second sailing.

You can fly direct to St Mary's Airport from Land's End, Newquay and Exeter airports by Skybus. If you're staying in one of the big hotels they will usually meet you and your luggage when you arrive. There are taxis and a shuttle bus from St Mary's Airport to Hugh Town.
T: (01736) 334220
www.islesofscilly-travel.co.uk

GETTING AROUND THE ISLANDS

St Mary's ferries

Ferries run to the inhabited islands throughout the year. There's a reduced service out of season and then you'll probably need to book. Off-island ferries usually start leaving Hugh Town Quay at about 10.15am with returns throughout the afternoon. Departure times and frequency change according to the tides, weather and time of year so check departure boards and social media accounts. Buy your ticket at the kiosk on Hugh Town Quay or on board.

Off-island ferries

If you're staying on an off-island, it will have its own boat service. They will run daily services to St Mary's plus a rotating mix of circular and evening trips throughout the week. In addition to their main ferry, most also have a smaller jet boat used for private charter.

Sightseeing boat trips

CIRCULAR TRIPS

All the island boat services offer circular trips around the uninhabited islands. With the exception of Samson, these don't land but afterwards you can usually land on one of the off-islands to stretch your legs, get a cup of tea and return on a later boat. Details are chalked on departure boards and on social media accounts.

Lowertown Quay, St Martin's

Samson

The only uninhabited island where ferries regularly land and a highlight of many holidays on Scilly. Abandoned houses still stand along with many prehistoric tombs on the hill tops. Prehistoric field walls cross the sand flats. Remember to take water, sun cream and a picnic with you.

Eastern Isles

Probably the most popular of the circular trips and usually the one with the calmest sea conditions. Great for getting close to grey seals who haul themselves out on Little Innisvouls. Seabirds nest on the steeper rocks. Private charter boats can drop you on Nornour or Arthur Quay.
Duration: 1¾ hours
Also lands on: St Martin's

Annet, Western Rocks and the Bishop

A trip to the far southwest of Scilly. Of all the boat trips, this is the one most dependent on sea conditions. If they're not right this trip might not run for a week or more – so it's best to go while you have the opportunity. If it's too rough to go all the way to the Bishop Rock Lighthouse, a shorter 1¼ hour trip may run to Annet for seals and seabirds.
Duration: 2½ hours
Also lands on: St Agnes

Norrard Rocks

A trip to the rocks and reefs to the west of Samson and Bryher – Illiswilgig, Scilly Rock and the Garden of the Maiden Bower. Grey seals and puffins.
Duration: 1½ hours
Also lands on: Bryher/Tresco

Holy Isles and Round Island Lighthouse

Islands that make up the northern edge of Scilly between Tresco and St Martin's. Round Island with its lighthouse, St Helen's, Teän. Puffins on Men-a-vaur. Private charter boats can drop you on St Helen's or Teän.
Duration: 1½ hours
Also lands on: Tresco, Bryher or St Martin's

St Mary's circular

A trip around the whole island. A taste of the open sea and coming in close to some of the bays and inlets like Porth Hellick and Pelistry.
Duration: 1¼ hours

Gig Racing

Follow the island gig races. Women race on Wednesday evenings and men on Friday evenings. The courses vary and trips often end up in an off-island pub.

Seabird Specials

Various trips throughout the year in different parts of Scilly to make the most of when seabirds are around. Includes evening trips to catch the return of shearwaters and puffins when they come back to Annet after a day fishing at sea. Puffins are around April to July, shearwaters stay a few weeks later and passing migrants arrive in spring and autumn. Often with commentary by a local bird expert.

Ancient Scilly

Sit back and hear about the history and archaeology of Scilly with an expert on-board commentary, as you cruise the islands.

95

Index